bondgirls*areforever*

bond girls are forever

THE WOMEN OF JAMES BOND

Maryam d'Abo   John Cork

Editorial Consultant Tim Greaves

Harry N. Abrams, Inc., Publishers

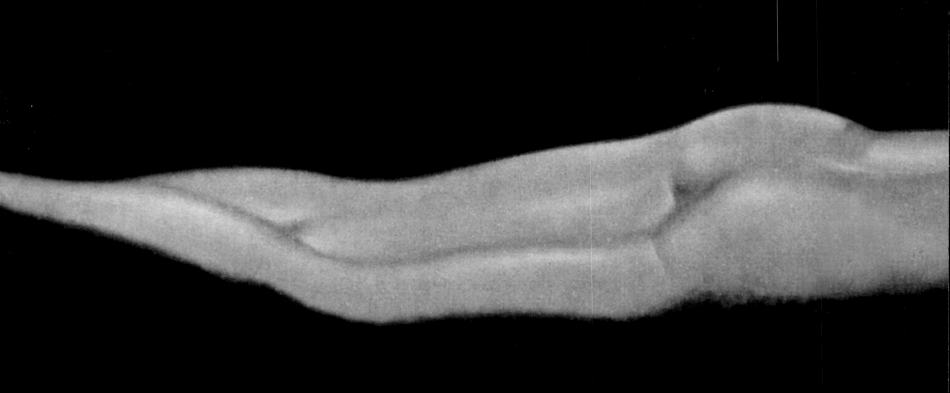

Library of Congress Cataloging-in-Publication Data

Cork, John.
  Bond girls are forever / John Cork and Maryam d'Abo.
    p. cm.
Includes bibliographical references and index.
  ISBN 0-8109-4302-6
  1. James Bond films. 2. Women in motion pictures. I. d'Abo, Maryam.
II. Title.

  PN1995.9.J3C67 2003
  791.43'652042'0973–dc21
                    2003012796

First published in 2003 by Boxtree, an imprint of Pan Macmillan, Ltd., London

Published in 2003 by Harry N. Abrams, Incorporated, New York. All rights reserved. No part of
the contents of this book may be reproduced without written permission of the publisher.

Printed and bound by the Bath Press, United Kingdom

Designed by Dave Breen

10 9 8 7 6 5 4 3 2 1

Harry N. Abrams, Inc.
100 Fifth Avenue
New York, N.Y. 10011
www.abramsbooks.com

Abrams is a subsidiary of

LA MARTINIÈRE
G R O U P E

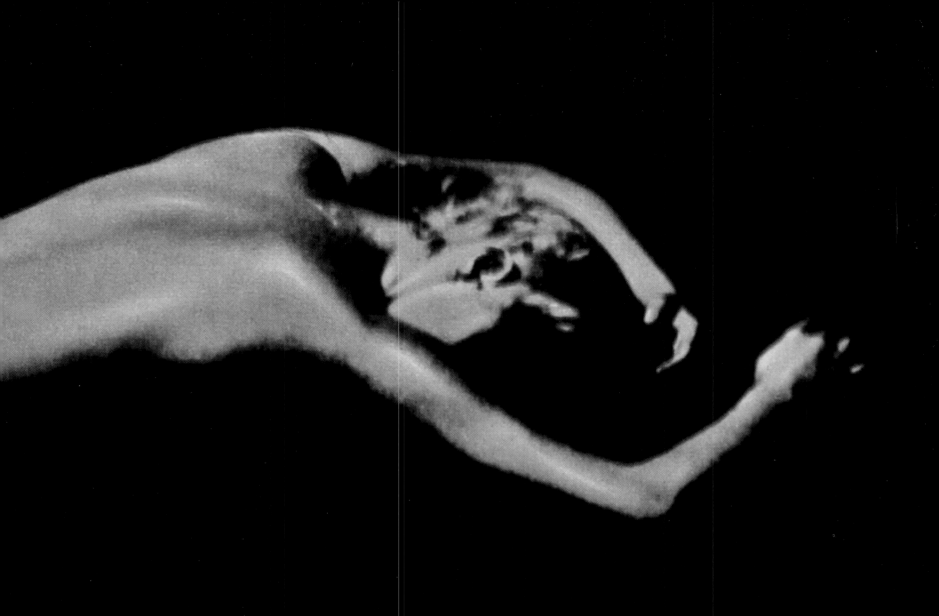

CONTENTS

FOREWORD
BEING A BOND GIRL – THE ILLUSION AND THE REALITY

In 1999, I travelled to Manhattan to pose for a unique photoshoot. Photographer Annie Leibovitz gathered eighteen women, all of whom, like me, had appeared in a James Bond movie. As with most things associated with 007, there was more and less to the final image that appeared in *Vanity Fair* magazine than met the eye. The actresses posed in two different studios on two sides of the United States on two different days. Annie and her team digitally merged numerous separate photos to create the final illusion of unity.

Being a Bond Girl is like posing for the Leibovitz photo. There is the reality, and there is the illusion so artfully created. Sometimes, even for those of us who were in the films, the line between reality and illusion is not so clear. Even though we were never in the same room, every Bond Girl who took part in the *Vanity Fair* shoot felt the special connection that exists between us all. It seemed as if we were all there together. The experience of gathering with my fellow actresses led me to wonder about the illusion and reality of being a Bond Girl. What did it mean? How had the experience changed us? How had our roles changed during the years? How had we changed the way women are viewed in films, if at all?

Those thoughts stuck with me, and I eventually produced a documentary on the subject, entitled, like this book, *Bond Girls Are Forever*. Making that film, I had the chance to talk in depth with a cross-section of the Bond actresses – from Ursula Andress to Halle Berry – and we were able to share our perspectives and feelings.

This book grew out of that documentary. Within these pages we hope to pull back the veil, to peer in at the illusion and the reality, to meet again the women of Bond's fictional world as well as the actresses who made them so memorable. We look at the history of the Bond Girls and how those fictional characters fit into the changing roles of women in society. We explore the magical allure the Bond women hold for both men and women. We meet the stars and hear from them how they came to the world of Bond and what it was like to make a Bond film. Finally, we reveal the impact the fictional realm of James Bond has had on the lives of those of us who have helped create it. Along the way, we have illustrated our story with rare images of some of the most beautiful women to grace movie screens.

It has been an adventure revisiting the past, meeting my counterparts, reassessing the role of women in the James Bond saga. For me, the journey was compelling and extraordinary.

Maryam d'Abo

Maryam d'Abo: 'This is a photo from my modelling days in the Eighties. With this photo, I felt I really jelled with the photographer. I didn't like working as a model that much. I liked it when I had a connection with a photographer, but I did not enjoy the cattle call for modelling jobs. When you leave a modelling shoot you don't feel enriched. When you leave a movie set after a day's filming, you feel inspired.'

INTRODUCTION

SOMEWHERE IN THE WORLD the sun is shining on a tropical beach. A man is gazing at a clear horizon where the turquoise waves touch an azure sky. In his mind everything is perfect except for one missing ingredient. Honey Ryder is not walking up on to the sand.

Somewhere, a woman is swimming in the sea feeling at one with the water. Her hair is wet, her make-up gone, and she could not care less. She feels healthy, beautiful and confident. She knows when she walks up on the beach, she will be back in a world where she will be expected to behave in a certain way, expected to dress, court, and even love according to the peculiar customs of the here and now. As she stands on the soft sands, the waves lapping around her calves, she thinks, 'If I could only carry this feeling with me forever. If only the rest of the world wouldn't mess with me. If only I could be wearing that belt with that knife slung on my hip. If only I could be like Ursula Andress in *Dr. No*.'

I was not present when Ursula Andress stepped from the Caribbean Sea on to the sands of Laughing Waters beach in Jamaica. I do remember the day after *Dr. No* was first broadcast on television. On Monday, 11 November, 1974, there was a palpable sense among my thirteen-year-old peers that we had all experienced an epiphany the night before.

'The image of Ursula Andress is bigger than life,' says Halle Berry, the Oscar-winning actress and star of the twentieth official Bond film, *Die Another Day*. She is not alone in her observation. Virtually every man and woman associated with the Bond movies cites the scene of Honey Ryder walking from the sea as a defining moment in cinema. It is producer Barbara Broccoli's quintessential image of a Bond Girl. When asked why, Broccoli, who is also far too young to remember the filming or release of *Dr. No* in 1962, says, 'I think, obviously, at that time, Ursula's whole look was very different from women that had come before. It was a very athletic, very strong, physical look. She meant business, and she is so stunningly beautiful.'

The Bond films are filled with memorable images of women. From the fighting gypsy girls in *From Russia With Love*, to Jill Masterson's golden corpse in *Goldfinger*, to Xenia Onatopp flashing a challenging smile as she roars past Bond in a red Ferrari in *GoldenEye*, the Bond Girls have never failed to raise viewers' heart rates.

Why does the world love the Bond Girls?

Is it just the physical beauty of the actresses? No one would argue that some of the most beautiful women in the world have appeared in the Bond films, but the world is filled with beautiful women. Movies, television and magazines provide a steady stream of images of heartbreaking faces and perfect figures.

Bond has no monopoly on beautiful women, and anyway, the attraction obviously goes beyond the surface. Beauty, according to the cliché, is only skin deep, and every man and woman has their preconceived ideas about it. If all the Bond Girls looked like carbon copies of Ursula Andress, it would be one thing. They do not. They defy any physical stereotype. There is a fair share of Nordic beauties but an equal number from Southern Europe. They have come from Africa, Canada, Poland, Japan, China, Yugoslavia, Malaysia, Ireland, the Caribbean, Israel and India. They have been fair and dark, short and tall, polished and wild. Some have had curves while others have been lean and toned. There are no set physical criteria for being a Bond Girl. Their beauty is not of a type. No, the recipe for a Bond Girl is more complex than good looks.

Having now met dozens of Bond Girls, pored over dozens more interview transcripts and seen the Bond films themselves more times than I can count, I can offer only one essential ingredient common to all these women. They all have far more to offer than meets the eye. This is true of many of the fictional Bond Girls, but absolutely true of the actresses who have played those memorable roles.

For me, working on this book has ignited very different emotions to those I experienced in 1974 when I first saw *Dr. No*. The Bond Girls are no less remarkable to me, but they are now something more than just a fantasy. They are wonderfully real, complex, human, yet every bit as amazing. This is their story – the characters they played, the world they lived in, the adventures they had and the challenges they faced.

John Cork

Ursula Andress in the scene that made her famous.

1 HISTORY

SHE IS, NATURALLY ENOUGH, BEAUTIFUL.

More importantly, she is independent, defiant, and probably dangerous. She has broken away from the location of her birth, venturing fearlessly into the wider world. She is searching for something, a sense of exhilaration, adventure, risk. The odds are that somewhere she took a wrong turn, met the wrong man and endured the wrong personal tragedy. Now, she has found herself in one of life's dark cul-de-sacs.

Then she meets him, the secret agent, the man who is only a silhouette, the man known as 007. He will give her his name and when she meets him, she knows at once that her fate has been sealed. She will risk it all, live life to the full, and fight. And after he has gone, she will remain in body and spirit part of an elite sisterhood. She will have become a Bond Girl.

This book is a tribute to one of the lasting icons of feminine strength, beauty and resilience of the past half-century – the James Bond woman. They are at once of a type and yet decidedly individual. And, despite the popular conception, they are anything but subservient to 007.

We remember the names Honey Ryder, Pussy Galore, Tiffany Case, Holly Goodhead, Jinx. We remember the adventures – the underwater battles, the narrow escapes on skis and in high-performance sports cars. But most of all we remember the vibrant sexual tension, the unashamed animal attraction, the looks that pass between a man and a woman most of us experience only a handful of times during our lives. It is this moment that seduces us – when Honey Ryder's eyes defiantly lock with James Bond's on the small beach at Crab Key. In that moment both men and women want to live in Bond's world, want to experience those thrills.

It is the casting of the Bond women that garners the most attention in the press during the pre-production of each film. When the film is released, the Bond movie posters contain two essential iconic images – a gun, and a beautiful woman. There have been Bond films without megalomaniac villains, without Q's gadgets, but there has never been a Bond film without a Bond woman.

Who are these women who have set styles and bucked trends? Long-time Bond screenwriter Richard Maibaum said the Bond Girls 'have become fantasy figures arousing powerful empathic responses in both sexes'. Why has this happened? Where did they come from? Where have they taken us? To understand the cinematic phenomenon of the Bond Girls, one must first explore the women of Bond's literary roots. That journey began just over six years after the end of the Second World War in the Fifties.

Maryam d'Abo

Honor Blackman on playing Pussy Galore: 'It's so strange. When I did the film, it was just a film. It was lovely working with Sean. I wouldn't pretend otherwise. But who would guess that it would have such a future?'

THE FIFTIES

The novels

WE CAN BLAME IT ALL ON A MAN. Ian Fleming, a former Naval Commander, stockbroker, journalist, adventurer and *bon vivant*, not only created James Bond, but also brought to life the Bond woman. She was something quite new in 1953 when Jonathan Cape published *Casino Royale*, the first of Fleming's twelve James Bond novels and nine short stories. Fleming gave his first Bond woman the name Vesper Lynd, and she stands at the head of a remarkable lineage of strong-willed, elegant women who have enchanted readers and movie-goers for the past half-century.

It is easy to point out that Vesper is quite different from some of the more recent athletic, hell-on-wheels Bond women like Wai Lin and Jinx, but her essential qualities have helped shape every Bond woman that followed her. She is beautiful, smart and dangerous. She may not run around assassinating enemy agents, but her actions bring James Bond closer to death than any woman who has followed. Bond realizes he can never fully know her, yet he falls in love with her and wants to marry her. It is through the tragic circumstances that surround the end of her life that Bond becomes the cold, ruthless secret agent the world knows so well.

Who is Vesper Lynd? She is a product of her times, but Fleming gives her qualities that make her timeless. She works for the British Secret Service, 'a wireless expert ... [who] speaks French like a native and knows her job backwards.' In short, she is intelligent and certainly not naïve. 'It goes without saying that Vesper is of a certain class,' observes Peter Janson-Smith, who served as Ian Fleming's agent, and, later, as the chairman of the company that controls Fleming's literary rights. 'In those days, of course, the women working for MI5 and MI6 were very much upper-class ladies. There were a lot of them actually from the aristocracy. Because if you took the daughter or granddaughter of this duke or that lord then she would have been brought up in such a way that you wouldn't have worried whether she would be discreet and loyal and safe.'

Writer Andrea Lee, who read the Bond novels in the late Sixties, agrees. The Bond women like Vesper, she feels, were 'not simple sexpots, but ruling-class goddesses.' Fleming elevated the Bond women to this status by describing their tastes with, as Lee says, 'fetishistic meticulousness.'

> Her hair was very black and she wore it cut square and low on the nape of the neck, framing her face to below the clear and beautiful line of her jaw. Although it was heavy and moved with the movements of her head, she did not constantly pat it back into place, but let it alone. Her eyes were wide apart and deep blue and they gazed candidly back at Bond with a touch of ironical disinterest which, to his annoyance, he found he would like to shatter, roughly. Her skin was lightly suntanned and bore no trace of make-up except on her mouth which was wide and sensual. Her bare arms and hands had a quality of repose and the general impression of restraint in her appearance and movements was carried even to her finger-nails which were unpainted and cut short. Round her neck she wore a plain gold chain of wide flat links and on the fourth finger on the right hand a broad topaz ring. Her medium length dress was of grey 'soie sauvage' with a square-cut bodice, lasciviously tight across her fine breasts. The skirt was closely pleated and flowed down from a narrow, but not a thin, waist. She wore a three-inch, hand-stitched black belt. A hand-stitched black 'sabretache' rested on the

A late-Fifties Pan edition paperback of *Casino Royale*. The artist was Peff, aka Sam Peffer.

LIVE AND LET DIE
Ian Fleming

chair beside her, together with a wide cartwheel hat of gold
straw, its crown encircled by a thin black velvet ribbon which
tied at the back in a short bow. Her shoes were square-toed of
plain black leather.

The readers of *Casino Royale*, or the later Bond novels, did not have to know what 'soie sauvage' is (a roughly woven cloth of raw silk), or a 'sabretache' (a leather purse designed in the style of a nineteenth-century cavalry saddle case) to understand that Ian Fleming's world was a more refined place than post-war London circa 1953.

Nonetheless, 1953 proved to be a perfect time to introduce a woman like Vesper to British readers. Queen Elizabeth ascended to the throne, and the growing British middle class was finally pulling out of the post-war gloom that had gripped the nation for so many years. They wanted to read about elegance, style and taste. They wanted to imagine sexual adventures in French casinos even if currency restrictions prevented most from leaving the country with enough money to indulge in Bond's high-stakes gaming. John Sutherland, in his history of British bestsellers, *Reading the Decades*, observes that television broadcasts 'signed off ... at ten o'clock; radio an hour later. Casinos were as unknown in Britain as opium dens ... Fewer than one in ten thousand would have ever visited a European casino.'

Vesper is not the quintessential Bond woman. She is a reluctant double agent, manipulated by the Soviets who have her former lover imprisoned under threat of death if she does not betray secrets. Ultimately, after she falls in love with Bond and realizes she has no escape from the predicament in which she finds herself, she commits suicide.

Vesper's alter ego was brought to life in 1954 by actress Linda Christian in the CBS television production of *Casino Royale* for the US anthology series Climax!. Christian played Valerie Mathis, an elegant temptress and former flame of Bond's who is also a double agent. This time, though, she is pretending to work for the Soviets and the villain LeChiffre but is really serving the French. Bond, for the record, is American, 'a member of Combined Intelligence'. Mathis aids Bond by advancing him money that he uses to defeat LeChiffre.

Despite the failure of the television production of *Casino Royale* to ignite much interest in James Bond, the impact of Ian Fleming's first novel on popular fiction cannot be underestimated. Yet, in a very important way, Fleming's treatment of Vesper is in line with the way women were portrayed in popular literature and movies of the day. Vesper and Bond enjoy a premarital affair that ends with tragic consequences. One can look at film after film, novel after novel from the period and see the pattern – women who were independent, sexual and self-determined did not end up living happily ever after, if they ended up living at all.

Examples of this moral code from the early Fifties can be found everywhere. In Graham Greene's classic 1951 novel *The End of the Affair*, a woman makes a deal with God that if her lover survives a bomb attack during the Second World War, she will never cheat on her husband again. A year and a half later, she breaks her vow with horrifying results. The most popular novel and film of the time was James Jones's *From Here to Eternity*, which was considered daringly sexually explicit for its day. It also featured women who paid a high price for their affairs. The film version, which won the Best Picture Oscar in 1953, starred the usually demure Donna Reed playing a prostitute and Deborah Kerr (who would later appear in 1967's film version of *Casino Royale*) as the neglected and unfaithful wife of an Army captain. Everyone has seen Kerr and Burt Lancaster embracing on the beach as the surf crashes over their bodies, an image all the more scandalous since Kerr's character was married to another man. But, in typical fashion, the Fifties morality took its toll on the liaison with a final denouncement – Kerr's character having to return to her loveless marriage.

Some critics have argued that this was a temporary shift in moral tone as a result of the baby boom in the US and Great Britain, and a societal emphasis on families after the chaos of war. They point to examples of earlier fiction with seductresses, fallen women, and *femme fatales* by authors like Eric Ambler, Dashiel Hammett, Raymond Chandler, and James M. Cain. These authors certainly knew how to lace their writing with a decadent sensuality, but there was always an air of moral rot evident in the characters and the telling of the tales. They, too, conformed to a code that condemned female sexuality, even as it exploited it.

As if in response to the type of moral balancing act that appeared throughout popular culture of the early Fifties, a young publisher decided to start a new kind of magazine. Launched in December 1953, it would be a publication that would have a long association with both Bond and many Bond women. The publisher's goal was 'to form a pleasure-primer styled to the masculine taste'. Hugh Hefner designed *Playboy* for men who enjoyed their 'entertainment served up with humour, sophistication and spice'. *Playboy* filled a void in publishing, launching a new voice that celebrated uncomplicated and uncommitted sex. *Playboy*'s success, at least in the US, illustrated the fact that attitudes about portraying women as sexually independent might be changing.

The year of Bond's birth was filled with other rumblings of the oncoming sexual revolution. Those rumblings were often as confusing as they were alarming. In Denmark, a man underwent the first sex change operation, Christian Dior raised hemlines to fifteen and a half inches above the ground on women's dresses, and Dr Alfred Kinsey released his landmark report, *Sexual Behavior in the Human Female*. Another influential book also gained notoriety – Ashley Montague's

Solitaire, as portrayed on the front of this vintage Pan edition of *Live and Let Die*, shows little of the confidence and sexual self-assurance that Fleming instilled in the women of his novels. In contrast, on the cinema posters, the filmmakers more often than not chose to show the Bond women as strong and independent.

FROM RUSSIA, WITH LOVE
Ian Fleming

Death-trap
for
James Bond

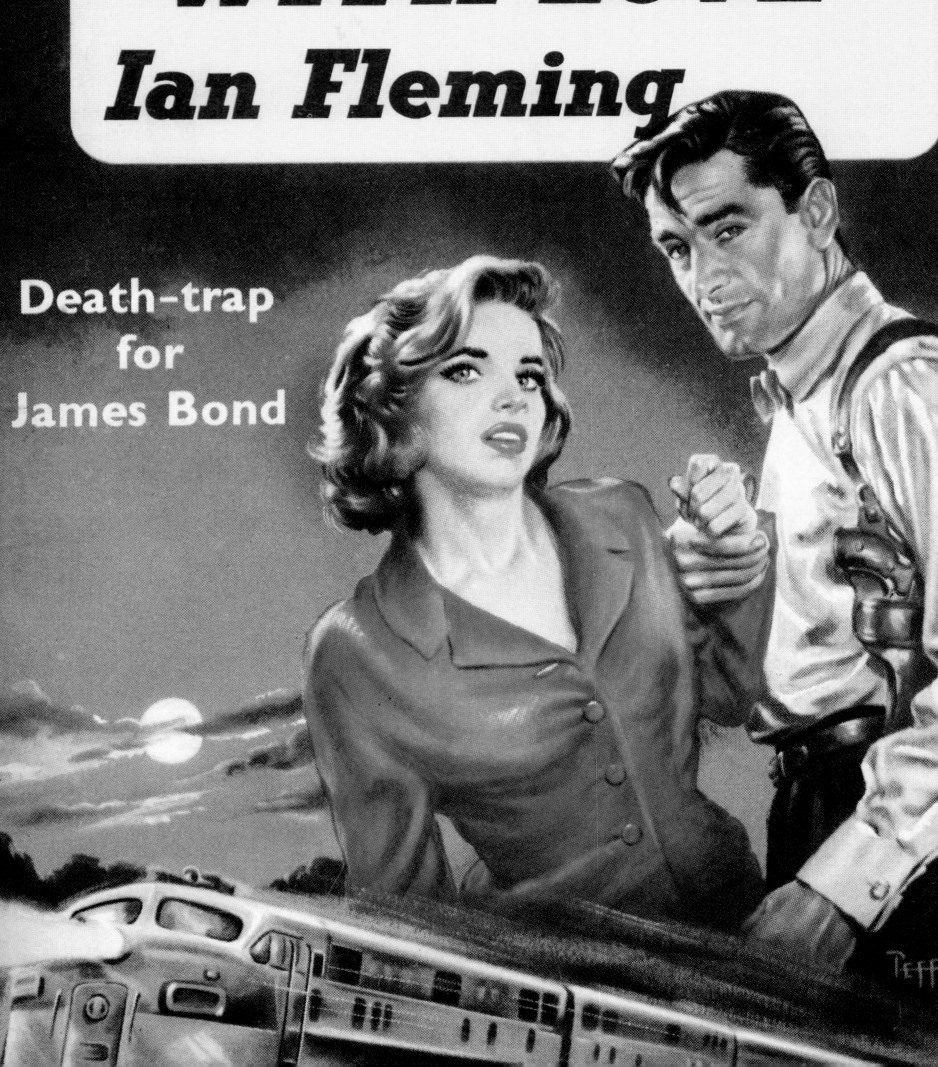

The Natural Superiority of Women, cited by many as the first volley in the post-war feminist movement. Nonetheless, the real role of women in society seemed to be shrinking. Women were getting married and having children earlier. Fewer were seeking college educations. In the US, the employment rate for women dropped below levels seen during the Great Depression in the Thirties.

By the time *Playboy* hit the stands in the US, Ian Fleming had long since written his second Bond novel, which was published in April 1954 under the title *Live and Let Die*. It was the character of Solitaire in this book that set the tone for what we think of as the Bond woman. Solitaire proved to be absolutely in touch with the burgeoning sexual revolution.

'Send in Miss Solitaire,' Mr Big intones. James Bond watches as 'one of the most beautiful women Bond had ever seen' enters the room.

> *The eyes were blue, alight and disdainful, but, as they gazed into his with a touch of humour, he realized they contained some message for him personally. It quickly vanished as his own eyes answered … Part of the beauty of her face lay in its lack of compromise. It was the face born to command. The face of the daughter of a French Colonial slave-owner … She watched his eyes on her and nonchalantly drew her forearms together in her lap so that the valley between her breasts deepened.*
>
> *The message was unmistakable…*

Strong, exotic, sexually aware, Solitaire was the kind of woman who simply did not appear in the popular literature of the day, at least not as a good girl. Ian Fleming happily tossed aside those moral conventions. He knew every woman harboured a bit of the rebel spirit beneath her wool skirt and twin set, and every man was hopelessly attracted to the promise of guilt-free sexual indulgence. Fleming celebrated the bad girl image without excuses. With Solitaire, he made the bad girl good.

'It is fun for me to be able to tease such a strong silent man,' a nude and flirtatious Solitaire taunts Bond barely twenty-four hours after they meet. There is no moral retribution for this kind of behaviour in Fleming's writings. The novel ends with Bond and Solitaire anticipating a libidinous fortnight together after their adventure. Neither appears to hold any illusions about a future beyond. Neither carries any guilt or any emotional burden as a consequence of their actions. Readers could enjoy the ride without having to worry about the author forcing atonement at the end.

'I think Fleming was on his own there,' notes Peter Janson-Smith. 'I don't think many authors were writing women that way at the time, if any.'

If Solitaire provided the first incarnation of the sexually liberated heroine, the model did not instantly stick with Fleming. His third 007

novel, *Moonraker*, featured Gala Brand, an attractive Special Branch agent. When the mission is over, Bond's erotic hopes are dashed. Miss Brand, it turns out, is to be married the following afternoon.

With the fourth Bond novel, *Diamonds Are Forever*, Fleming is back in the territory of the good/bad girl with the diamond-smuggling Tiffany Case. Her character, though, is decidedly complex. The daughter of a San Francisco madam, she was gang-raped at sixteen and later nearly killed herself with alcohol. To survive, she forged a rock-hard exterior. Nonetheless, the mutual seduction – on the transatlantic run of the *Queen Elizabeth* – involves far more than just sex. James debates the wisdom of involvement: 'Bond knew that he was very near to being in love with her … But was he prepared for the consequences? Once he had taken her by the hand it would be forever.' There is real emotional weight to the conversations and delicate negotiations between Bond and Tiffany, baggage that Fleming quickly shed at the beginning of his next novel, *From Russia With Love*. Through a meeting with Bond's boss, M, we learn that Tiffany has left 007 for a more stable relationship with a US Marine Corps major.

Fleming informs the reader, 'the last thing [M] wanted was for Bond to be permanently tied to one woman's skirts'. Thus, with the fifth James Bond novel, Fleming settles on the idea of Bond's affairs being brief and transitory. To accomplish this, Fleming created a series of characters more in the mould of Solitaire, women who pass their time with Bond like the proverbial ships in the night. Over the next few novels, Fleming indulged his readers with richly drawn Bond women – Tatiana Romanova, the Soviet translator assigned to seduce 007; the orphaned, self-reliant beachcomber, Honeychile Rider; Goldfinger's paid companion, Jill Masterton; and the female gang leader, Pussy Galore. Fleming had established a pattern accepted by his readership that did not entail the heroine of one adventure making the transition to another.

By the end of the decade, the die was cast. Cultural forces like Ian Fleming's Bond novels and *Playboy* magazine were reshaping the popular view of women. Fleming and *Playboy*'s influence were derided by some critics, but Fleming's novels received far more copious amounts of praise in the late Fifties. James Sandoe in the *New York Herald-Tribune Book Review* referred to *Dr. No* (1958) as 'The most artfully bold, dizzyingly poised thriller of the decade'. Just over a year earlier, the *Times Literary Supplement* proclaimed, 'James Bond's appeal is that he expresses the fantasies about power and sexual fulfilment felt by many who live under the twin shadows of Communism and the hydrogen bomb.' Even in Paul Johnson's famously snide review of *Dr. No*, his only criticism of the role of women is the complaint that the novel is filled with 'the mechanical, two-dimensional sex-longings of a frustrated adolescent'.

Little could Johnson have known that the appeal of the Bond Girls to frustrated adolescents around the world was only just beginning.

Peff's artwork is featured on this late-Fifties Pan edition of *From Russia With Love*. He always took care to paint Bond as described through Vesper Lynd's eyes in *Casino Royale*, 'He reminds me rather of Hoagy Carmichael, but there is something cold and ruthless.' Peff was noted for his ability to paint expressive eyes and his natural instinct for vivid colours. He claims that there was 'nothing political' in his choice to clothe Russian Tatiana Romanova in red, but the hue certainly gets the point across to the reader.

T H E   S I X T I E S

What can I write about the Sixties that hasn't been written? Everything was up for grabs – sex, society, politics, fashion. It was the decade when Honey Ryder walked out of the Caribbean Sea in her white bikini with a knife strapped to her hip – and, when a woman with a gun looked out from movie screens and said, 'My name is Pussy Galore.'

Just as James Bond was every man's fantasy of a cool warrior in the sexual revolution, the Bond Girls were equally recognized as harbingers of a new kind of femininity. They were strong, smart, beautiful, and carried themselves with assurance. They weren't just sexy – a term that applies to a sports car as much as it does to a woman.

The Bond Girls of the Sixties made their sexuality fun. You could hear cinema-goers saying, 'Move over Doris Day and Sandra Dee, the Bond Girls have arrived.' Bond Girls were everywhere: on television, in music, in advertising, in fashions. Doris Day ended up starring in her own brand of spy film, *The Glass Bottom Boat* (1966).

The Bond Girls were our fantasies of the times. The image of Jill Masterson's painted body in *Goldfinger* is on screen for less than a minute, but it was simply unforgettable in its perverse beauty. When James Bond and Domino sink behind a coral-head in *Thunderball* only to be followed by a cascade of bubbles rising up, it brought to mind dreams of near weightless lovemaking.

Even the sexist images are presented with such unabashed directness that they are more amusing than offensive. In *From Russia With Love*, a woman played by Jan Williams arrives to give Donald Grant (Robert Shaw) a massage. Before she starts, she inexplicably strips down to her bra and pants. In one sense, the moment is a droll parody of how the West viewed Soviet-style unemotional sexuality. In another, the scene simply offers the audience a better look at Williams's body. In *You Only Live Twice*, James Bond must undergo some kind of process to look more Japanese. The team of technicians gathered in the high-tech operating theatre for this procedure are none other than four bath girls wearing bikini tops and short shorts. As Jill St John said to me, 'It's a fantasy. How can anybody take that seriously and complain about it?'

The range of female characters in the Bond films of the decade was remarkably rich. The leading ladies had wonderfully entertaining interactions with James Bond and their journeys were unpredictable. In looking back on all the women in the Bond films, I am drawn most to the characters in the films of the Sixties. I find them extraordinary and full of humour.

Maryam d'Abo

'How did I get the role of Pussy Galore? It all sounds very immodest when I answer but, since I was the hottest thing in England at that time with *The Avengers*, and I did judo on the show, and Pussy Galore had to do judo, it was just a sidestep, really.' Honor Blackman on how she was cast in *Goldfinger*.

'I ADMIRE YOUR LUCK'

SYLVIA TRENCH TO JAMES BOND IN *DR. NO*

BY 1960, THE JAMES BOND novels had become a phenomenon in Britain. They were serialized in newspapers and transformed into comic strips. Despite the great success, numerous attempts to turn the novels into films or even adapt Bond for television failed.

Before Albert R 'Cubby' Broccoli and Harry Saltzman would make the first 007 film, Fleming published two more novels and a collection of short stories entitled *For Your Eyes Only*. The novels – *Thunderball* and *The Spy Who Loved Me* – feature increasingly memorable heroines.

In *Thunderball*, Fleming takes the reader into the world of Dominetta Vitali, the villain's mistress. In one chapter, she details a romantic fantasy involving the image of a sailor on the old Players cigarette packages. This beautifully drawn bit of writing seemed to be the practice run for Fleming's most bold literary experiment – *The Spy Who Loved Me* – where the entire novel is told from the perspective of Vivienne Michel, and much of it has to do with Michel's emotionally scarred past. The novel met with harsh reviews from many male critics, including a comment from James Price that became a precursor to the later feminist assaults on the Bond genre, that each Bond woman was nothing more than 'an animated pin-up, conceived purely as a sexual object'. In his detailed examination of the literary 007, *The James Bond Dossier*, Sir Kingsley Amis noted that female critics tended to embrace the book. Could it be that Ian Fleming, who is widely acknowledged as having his finger on the pulse of masculine desires, also had an equal ability to write for women?

Eunice Gayson (opposite, with Sean Connery) had worked with director Terence Young, producer Albert R. 'Cubby' Broccoli, and screenwriter Richard Maibaum before on *Zarak* (1956). When Young told her he wanted to cast her, he said, 'You always bring me luck in my films.'

Sean Connery and Ursula Andress (below) napping in the sun while shooting on Jamaica's idyllic North Shore near Ocho Rios.

'WOMEN LIKE THIS HAD SIMPLY NEVER BEEN SEEN IN FILMS BEFORE'

JOHN CORK

Martine Beswick (in the green) and Aliza Gur (in the red) played the fighting gypsy girls in *From Russia With Love*. The fight, as choreographed by stuntman Peter Perkins, was designed to be both thrilling and erotic.

Dr. No

In 1962, the year *Dr. No* was filmed and released in the United Kingdom, Stanley Kubrick premiered the controversial classic, *Lolita*, based on the widely praised and equally widely banned 1955 novel by Vladimir Nabokov. The film, detailing a pathetic affair between a grown man and a pubescent girl, heralded a new attitude by major Hollywood studios towards material formerly deemed inappropriate for mainstream movies. The publication and tremendous popularity of Helen Gurley Brown's book, *Sex and the Single Girl*, mocked the notion of most unmarried women waiting for marriage and gave cultural approval for a generation of young women to experiment with sex before making a life commitment.

The recent introduction of the birth control pill in Britain and the US heralded a major change for women and men and the role of sex in society. If *Playboy* and the Kinsey Institute reports on human sexuality had signalled the start of the sexual revolution, the introduction of the Pill marked the turning point in the war. In the world of films, the Pill represented the end of an era in the portrayal of women.

In the pre-Pill Fifties, Marilyn Monroe was the sex symbol *du jour*. Beautiful and sexually alluring, yet innocent, she perfectly captured the uneasy mix of unabashed feminine desire with the moral constraints of her day. With the introduction of the Pill it is almost as if society declared that the facade of 'girl next door' innocence could be dropped, that the old standards of moral acceptability no longer applied.

On 5 August 1962, two months prior to the London premiere of *Dr. No*, Marilyn Monroe took an overdose of barbiturates and died at her home. With her, the popular notions of sexuality in the Fifties died, too. It was a propitious moment for the cinematic birth of the Bond Girl.

However one wishes to define the success of *Dr. No*, sex is a key ingredient. This film has none of the trademark gadgets, no massive action set pieces, its musical score – except for the use of Monty Norman's 'The James Bond Theme' – doesn't even sound like the other James Bond films of the Sixties. *Dr. No* does, though, take place in a universe that can only be described as libidinous. The film begins with Bond being seduced by one woman and ends with him in the arms of another. Along the way, 007 openly flirts with the boss's secretary and beds an enemy agent. The use of sex in the film was nothing short of audacious.

Ursula Andress on filming in Jamaica: 'I met Noel Coward there. He told the most wonderful stories and had such a great sense of humour, and, of course, I got to know Ian Fleming with his *savoir faire* and his dignity. It was really incredible to meet all these people and be with them.' Here Andress talks with Fleming on the set at Laughing Waters beach in February, 1962.

'HE WAS ADORABLE TO ME.
IT WAS A PLEASURE TO KISS HIM.
A GREAT PLEASURE'

URSULA ANDRESS ON WORKING WITH SEAN CONNERY

'The world was quite different in the early Sixties when Bond arrived on the scene,' says Dana Broccoli, widow of Bond producer Cubby Broccoli. 'Bond women were nothing like the women in earlier films ... I think that the female audiences were welcoming the change as were the men.'

It is through the eyes of cinema's first Bond Girl that we first meet 007. Sylvia Trench (Eunice Gayson) is described in the screenplay for *Dr. No* as 'willowy, exquisitely gowned, with a classic, deceptively cold beauty.' In short, she is rich, gorgeous, and confident – the kind of woman men want to meet and women want to be. She comfortably plays *chemin de fer* for high stakes. She presents an unruffled exterior, even when Bond confronts her with a gun. Finally, she is sexually assured enough to break into James Bond's home and proposition him without seeming to demean herself. As Tim Greaves, author of *The Bond Women: 007 Style* (and editorial consultant on this book), notes, 'Back in 1962 good girls just didn't behave like this!'

Introducing James Bond through Sylvia Trench was a stroke of pure genius. Having a woman of such rarefied tastes hurl herself at 007, elevated Bond himself. Having her do so with such aplomb came down to the talents of the filmmakers.

Eunice Gayson recalls that director Terence Young thought the character would become part of the James Bond stock company. 'He said, "I think I'm going to do this new series of James Bond films, and I think it'll last for six films. [At the beginning of each film] you and James Bond are just about to get to it and he's always bleeped away, but in the sixth one, he isn't bleeped away, and you get him."' As it turned out, Sylvia Trench was herself bleeped away after the second Bond film, *From Russia With Love*.

Bond next meets Miss Taro (Zena Marshall), a secretary at Government House in Jamaica who is secretly part of Dr No's villainous network. 'I was trying to be this attractive little siren, and at the same time I was the spy, a bad woman,' remembers Zena Marshall. Miss Taro invites Bond to her apartment in the mountains but never expects him to arrive; it is a ruse to lure him into an assassin's trap. Bond eludes his killers and surprises Miss Taro at her home. Bond quickly deduces that Miss Taro is also in a trap. She must keep 007 at her home until another of the villain's operatives can come to kill him. Bond makes it clear that he only intends to stay if she sleeps with him.

After sex, Bond acts as if he is calling for a taxi to take them to dinner, but instead summons an unmarked police car. When the car arrives, Bond shoves Miss Taro inside. Miss Taro, now fully humiliated, spits in Bond's face. The scene is a twist on a long history of *femme fatales* and fallen women who lure men into traps with the promise of easy sex. Invariably, the man is at the woman's mercy. In James Bond's universe, it is Bond who seizes control, coldly manipulating the situation so that it is the villainess who finds herself played. Audiences in 1962 had never seen anything like this, and they loved it. Then they met Honey.

The entrance of Honey Ryder (Ursula Andress) in *Dr. No* ranks as one of the most famous images in film. She walks casually on to a beach in her white bikini, a belt with a sheathed diving knife resting against her hip. She tosses her shells and mask on the sand, softly singing a calypso tune, unselfconscious of her natural beauty and unaware that Bond is watching her. When Bond lets his presence be known, it is Honey who takes charge. She stands defiantly, shoulders back, ready to fight. 'Stay where you are,' she commands.

'I promise I won't steal your shells,' Bond tells her.

'I promise you won't either,' Honey replies, a grimly confident note

in her voice. Bond steps forward again, and she whips out the knife from her diving belt. She will defend herself, and she is not afraid to resort to violence. Honey is another innocent caught up in Bond's adventure. She may not be a spy nor connected to the villain, but she is certainly strong enough and smart enough to be part of Bond's world.

She grew up with her father, a marine biologist specializing in shells, in places like the Philippines, Bali and Hawaii. She is self-taught, reading through most of a set of encyclopaedias for her informal education. After her father disappeared, Honey had to learn to fend for herself. She tells Bond how she killed a man who raped her by dropping a black widow spider into his bed. She is the one who knows the island well enough to get Bond away from the tracking dogs. She does not need Bond to save her except from the consequences of his actions.

At the film's end Bond and Honey float adrift in a boat, where they are located by Bond's CIA ally, Felix Leiter. Honey's stance beside Bond when they are found – like a captain at the prow of a ship – shows her continued strength and independence. While the film is a Bond movie, Honey is her own person, as fully drawn as Bond, and equally as resourceful.

The Bond Girls from *Dr. No* marked a new kind of woman in the cinema. Sylvia Trench, Miss Taro and Honey Ryder were strong-willed, resourceful, and sexually independent. They signalled the introduction not just of a new film hero, but a new generation of women who wanted and expected more out of life.

˙ Zena Marshall on playing Miss Taro: 'I was trying to be this attractive little siren at the same time I was the spy, a bad woman ... We cast the die for the whole series of Bond films. Very stylized ... The women were more exotic.'

'YOU'RE ONE OF THE MOST BEAUTIFUL GIRLS I'VE EVER SEEN'
'I THINK MY MOUTH IS TOO BIG'

JAMES BOND AND TATIANA ROMANOVA IN
FROM RUSSIA WITH LOVE

From Russia With Love

'We can no longer ignore that voice within women that says: "I want something more than my husband and my children and my home."'
Betty Friedan, *The Feminine Mystique* (1963)

The theme of women trapped in oppressive, suffocating situations fuelled the women's movement in the Sixties and Seventies. In a very different form, that same theme had played throughout the James Bond novels and it would run through many of the early Bond films, starting with *From Russia With Love*.

Despite the visual spice of belly dancing and fighting gypsy women, there is really only one Bond Girl in the second James Bond film, *From Russia With Love*. She is Corporal of State Security, Tatiana Romanava (Daniela Bianchi). SPECTRE (Special Executive for Counter-intelligence, Terrorism, Revenge and Extortion) utilizes Tatiana as a pawn in a plot to lure James Bond into a trap by seducing him.

Tatiana has none of the darkness of a traditional spy. She has an engaging, optimistic smile. She aspired to be a ballet dancer, 'but I grew an inch over regulation height'. When asked about her three lovers, she shrugs wistfully.

To bring Tatiana into the scheme, SPECTRE employs its Director of Operations, an ex-SMERSH Colonel, Rosa Klebb, aka Number Three (Lotte Lenya). Klebb is the anti-Bond woman, famously described as 'toad-like' by Ian Fleming in his novel. She is unattractive, severe, and nearly sexless until she reveals a potentially predatory lesbian desire. Klebb orders Romanova to seduce James Bond under the threat of death, to, as Klebb puts it, 'do anything he says'.

James Bond's first glimpse of Tatiana in the flesh is through the gauzy curtains of his hotel room. She is slipping into his bed, nude save for black stockings and a black choker around her neck. The image was right at the edge of acceptability when the film opened in the UK in 1963. Bond enters, gun in hand, wearing only a towel. The pair know they will sleep together that night, each believing they are working under orders of their government. It is an arranged marriage of sorts.

Bond introduces himself and shakes Tatiana's hand.

'You're one of the most beautiful girls I've ever seen,' he tells her. She smiles. 'Thank you. But I think my mouth is too big.'

James Bond looks at her mouth, shown glistening in close-up, and utters a double entendre that made those who understood it in 1963 nearly choke on their popcorn. 'No it's the right size. For me, that is.' The music comes in, Bond kisses Tatiana, and the audience knows that we need not worry about the awkward morality of the relationship. Sex in James Bond's world is, as Rosa Klebb says, 'a real labour of love'.

After the murder of Bond's friend, Kerim Bey, on board the Orient Express, Bond's trust in Tatiana is shattered. When he confronts her, Tatiana is truly ignorant of the killing. Bond spits out the word 'liar' in response, then hits her hard across the face. He immediately regrets the action as Tatiana pleads with him that she can say nothing until they are in England, even if he were willing to kill her. The genius of this scene is that the violence weakens Bond, and in its aftermath it is brilliantly unclear if even Tatiana believes her professions of love for Bond, while he himself is unable to ignore his emotions for her.

The scene is notable because it neither presents comic-book violence nor reflects other moments of uncomfortable physical coercion by Bond in other films. Whereas Bond used enemy agent Miss Taro for sport in *Dr. No*, he is emotionally conflicted about Tatiana. Future Bond producer Barbara Broccoli (who was a small child when her father produced *From Russia With Love*) says of Tatiana, 'I think she is an interesting character. I don't consider her a victim. She was exploited by her vicious, manipulative boss but in the end she gets out of the situation and heroically saves Bond's life.'

In fact, Tatiana not only rescues Bond but kills her controller, Colonel Klebb, in a Venice hotel suite. Through the taste of independence from her adventure with James Bond, she gains the inner conviction to choose freedom over fear.

Like Tatiana many women in the Bond films are transformed in the course of the story. They are not weak but trapped – usually by their association with the villain. It is Bond who often sees their potential, who offers them a glimpse of the world beyond, but these women usually have two fates – they either play a key role in bravely destroying the villain ... or they die.

'LOTTE WAS A VERY SMALL, VERY SWEET WOMAN. HER ROLE OF A TOUGH VILLAIN WAS JUST TOTALLY DIFFERENT FROM WHAT SHE WAS'

DANIELA BIANCHI (TATIANA ROMANOVA) ON LOTTE LENYA (ROSA KLEBB)

Blackman works with stuntman Bob Simmons on the dangerous summersault manoeuvre (opposite and above).

Goldfinger

By the third 007 film, *Goldfinger*, James Bond was already renowned for his ability to seduce women, and the filmmakers rightly embraced this with luxurious excess. In fact, *Goldfinger* features four significant women. The first is a *femme fatale* named Bonita (Nadja Regin), a tarantella dancer at the El Scorpio nightclub in Mexico. The scene is almost a reverse of the finale of *From Russia With Love*. Bonita also sees an assassin coming for Bond, but she does nothing to warn 007. Bond sees the reflection of the assassin in her eye and manages to spin her around so that she takes the blow.

It is important that the film starts with Bond's betrayal by a *femme fatale*, since during the story he seduces the two women closest to the villain. In Miami, Bond meets Jill Masterson (Shirley Eaton). Jill is serving unhappily as Auric Goldfinger's paid companion and card-cheating accomplice. When she departs Goldfinger's employment for Bond's hotel suite she pays the ultimate price. Famously, Goldfinger has her painted gold, suffocating her by blocking the pores of her skin. Jill becomes the first 'good girl' in the Bond films that James Bond cannot save.

Jill Masterson's death sends her sister Tilly (Tania Mallet) out on a mission of vengeance to kill Goldfinger. In the novel, Tilly survives until nearly the end of the story, competing for the reader's attention with the final Bond girl from *Goldfinger*. Fleming complained in a letter to his friend Ivar Bryce that he was having a hard time resolving the story with two women. The filmmakers, having witnessed Fleming's dilemma had no qualms about killing off Tilly early with Oddjob's metal-rimmed hat. They knew no other woman could share the screen with the Bond Girl with the most memorable name of them all – Pussy Galore (Honor Blackman).

In the film, Pussy Galore's lesbianism is toned down and her role expanded. She is now Goldfinger's personal pilot and runs an all-female stunt aerial show – Pussy Galore's Flying Circus. Her goal, apparently, is to become Honey Ryder. She confesses that she hopes to find a deserted island somewhere and go back to nature. To achieve this, Pussy agrees to have her pilots spray a dose of Delta 9 nerve gas over Fort Knox and the surrounding area.

A prisoner of Goldfinger's for the last half of the film, Bond tries many times to foil the villain's plan. The one tack that works is his rather violent seduction of Pussy Galore. In a scene that would be unlikely to appear in a film today, Bond and Pussy trade judo moves in a hay-filled barn, then Bond forces his weight upon her as she struggles to push him back. He plants a kiss on her and then she becomes as pliant as a feather pillow.

Scenes like this one were not uncommon in films. *Gone with the Wind* (1939) contains the most famous example with Rhett Butler forcibly carrying Scarlet O'Hara up the stairs to bed. The most egregious example appears in Sam Peckinpah's 1971 thriller *Straw Dogs* (edited by future Bond director Roger Spottiswoode), where a gang rape scene turns enjoyable for the victim. That movie's video release was banned in the UK in 1984 for the scene's explicit nature and reprehensible implications. Nonetheless, the scene in *Goldfinger* (like its counterpart in *Gone with the Wind*) still plays without noticeable objections from viewers of both sexes. Why?

Camille Paglia, the noted anti-feminist, takes a decidedly positive view of the barn scene in *Goldfinger*.

> *Feminists have always had trouble with this sort of, what they would regard as chauvinist and even quasi-violent behaviour in these heroes. And yet [James Bond and Rhett Butler] are some of the most charismatic men, truly virile men in the history of Hollywood ... The aspect of rough play in Sean Connery's behaviour with women on screen is, I think, part of the power. Those James Bond films – because of the incredible sexual tension, and the power of magnetism between the Bond Girls and James Bond – those films have never lost their sexual charge.*

It would be easy to dismiss Paglia's view if there was not an uncomfortable grain of truth in it, at least on a fantasy level.

Ultimately, the reasons Bond's 'seduction' of Pussy Galore succeeds in not offending viewers is the same reason Rhett Butler gets away with hauling off Scarlett O'Hara. These women are so strong, so independent, it seems implicit that they can't be raped. Paglia is right when she says, 'Pussy Galore played by Honor Blackman … is one of the most commanding, authoritative women in popular culture of the time.' Women like this have to be met with a force equal to their internal power. When Pussy Galore wrestles with Bond, she is, in a sense, wrestling with her own conflicting emotions.

There is another more subtle aspect to Bond's seduction of Pussy, particularly when he tells her that Goldfinger is 'quite mad'. One hopes that he also told her the truth about the nerve gas to be used in the raid. Delta 9, it turns out, is fatal. One doubts that Pussy Galore ever intended to be part of the mass murder of tens of thousands. Regardless, Bond plants enough seeds of doubt (pun intended) that Pussy eventually contacts the CIA and helps them switch the gas in the canisters, thus saving the day.

During the penultimate scene, Pussy Galore is still with Goldfinger, aiding him in kidnapping Bond aboard a presidential jet. It is reasonable to ask why by the end she hasn't ditched Goldfinger or turned him over to the authorities, but no one ever does. Her strength, autonomy and self-confidence don't allow an audience to second guess her motives or actions. It is those qualities that make her character so memorable. She is the first Bond woman who is Bond's equal in virtually every aspect. She can fight, make love, seduce, and scheme right alongside 007. She is, like her name, unique.

The Last Fleming Bond Novels
Between the premiere of *Dr. No* and *Goldfinger*, Ian Fleming published two more novels (*On Her Majesty's Secret Service* and *You Only Live Twice*). His final novel, *The Man With The Golden Gun*, would be published posthumously. In those three books, Fleming continued to draw exotic heroines for Bond's adventures, but each – La Comtessa Teresa di Vicenzo, Kissy Suzuki, and Mary Goodnight – seem more domestic in a way, more like partners in Bond's adventures than icons to be saved and possessed.

Although *On Her Majesty's Secret Service* ends in tragedy with the assassination of Tracy, James Bond does marry her. His reasons are clear:

> She's adventurous, brave, resourceful. She's exciting always. She seems to love me. She'd let me go on with my life. She's a lone girl, not cluttered up with friends, relations, belongings. Above all, she needs me. It'll be someone for me to look after. I'm fed up with all these untidy, casual affairs that leave me with a bad conscience.

Bond is emotionally shattered at the opening of *You Only Live Twice*, lost in grief over the death of Tracy. He is sent on a mission to Japan, which seems simple at first, but turns out to be one of his most challenging. He is forced to confront Ernst Stavro Blofeld, the man who murdered his wife. Bond kills Blofeld, avenging Tracy's death, but during his escape, he loses his memory in a terrible fall. By the end of the novel he believes he is a fisherman whose life revolves around his lover Kissy and the small Japanese village where they live. He is pulled away from his idyllic world when he sees a familiar word, 'Vladivostok', and realizes that it leads to a connection with his forgotten past.

In Fleming's final Bond novel, 007 works with the former secretary of the '00' section, Mary Goodnight. By the end, she is offering Bond a room in her Jamaican home, and even to 'cook and sew a few buttons on.' Fleming does not have Bond recoil in horror at Goodnight's vision of domestic bliss. As he drew his literary history of 007 to a close, Ian Fleming has Bond noting that the offer is 'doom-fraught' and 'insidious, the most deadly', nonetheless, it is one James Bond accepts. 'He said, and meant it, "Goodnight. You're an angel."'

Ian Fleming died on 12 August, 1964, slightly more than one month before the London opening of *Goldfinger*. He was only fifty-six years old. Later that day, an eleven-year-old boy arrived in London from Ireland. His name was Pierce Brosnan.

Tania Mallet (Tilly Masterson) was one of Britain's top models in the Sixties. She was strongly considered for the role of Tatiana Romanova in *From Russia With Love*, and in fact her mother was Russian. Mallet did not enjoy acting and decided to concentrate on modelling after *Goldfinger*. She has been active in charity work, helping to organize the Oxfam arts council in 1963.

Thunderball

Thunderball offered a trio of memorable Bond Girls. The first is a character totally uninvolved in Bond's milieu, an osteopath named Patricia Fearing (Mollie Peters). Although Pat (as she is called in the film) does not play much of a role in the story, she is the kind of woman whom Bond finds attractive. She is smart, strong, and a trained professional in a then innovative field of alternative medicine (not merely a nurse as she is often described). She is, in fact, the only professional whom Bond deals with at the clinic. As Fleming wrote in the novel, she possesses 'a hint of authority that would be a challenge to men'.

The character who proves to be a more formidable challenge to men is Fiona Volpe (Luciana Paluzzi), chief executioner for SPECTRE, a fiery redhead who sleeps with men as casually as she kills them. Bond finally meets Fiona in Nassau on the trail of two stolen atomic weapons. The pair seem barely able to contain the sexual sparks before sleeping together, after which they immediately start trying to kill each other.

The heroine of *Thunderball* is Dominique Derval (Claudine Auger) the sister of a murdered French Air Force commandant, and the mistress of the film's villain, Emilio Largo. Her friends call her Domino, a name that implies a hidden identity.

Like Jill Masterson in *Goldfinger*, Bond's seduction puts Domino at great risk. She is tortured when Largo discovers she has betrayed him. After Bond foils Largo's attempt to plant one atomic bomb in Biscayne Bay, Bond climbs aboard Largo's speeding hydrofoil, where the last bomb remains. At the end of a brutal fight scene, Largo levels a gun at Bond, but before he can fire, Domino shoots him in the back with a spear gun. 'I'm glad I killed him', she says with bitterness.

'*You're* glad?' Bond asks rhetorically. Once again, it is the Bond Girl who saves Bond's life and kills the villain.

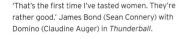

'That's the first time I've tasted women. They're rather good.' James Bond (Sean Connery) with Domino (Claudine Auger) in *Thunderball*.

'I THINK I WILL ENJOY VERY MUCH SERVING UNDER YOU'

AKI (AKIKO WAKABAYASHI) TO JAMES BOND
IN *YOU ONLY LIVE TWICE*

You Only Live Twice and *Casino Royale*

Just before the release of *You Only Live Twice*, another Bond film, *Casino Royale* opened in cinemas. *Casino Royale* was filmed under rights not controlled at that time by Bond producers Cubby Broccoli and Harry Saltzman. It had precious little to do with the novel of the same name, and was nothing if not opulent. It was also incomprehensible, and filled with an excess of beautiful women, variously mocking and embracing the spy chick chic of the mid-Sixties. At every turn in *Casino Royale* beautiful women cast enticing looks at virtually every male character. It even featured Ursula Andress as Vesper Lynd, reinvented as the world's richest woman.

By the end of *Thunderball*, three of the four types of women who appear so often as Bond Girls had graced the screen. There were the naïve beauties like Sylvia Trench and Patricia Fearing who had no direct connection to the world of espionage, the *femme fatales* like Miss Taro and Fiona Volpe, and the 'angels with a wing down' like Tatiana Romanova, Jill Masterson, and Domino who were held under the thumb of a villain. With the next EON-produced Bond film, audiences would meet the last type of woman that rounds out Bond's universe – the comrade-in-arms. These are women who are Bond's allies, who are often on the same or similar missions to Bond. They usually have the best chance of matching Bond's spy skills, and 007 is obviously attracted by the challenge they present to him.

Whereas the Bond films based on Fleming's books had presented richly characterized, independent women, the parodies and spoofs of Bond had turned 007's easy-going sexual morality into a joke. Matt Helm movies starring Dean Martin were filled with Thirties-style sexpots and leering vaudeville humour. James Coburn's Derek Flint maintained a harem of four women at his apartment to cater to his needs. Some complained that the Bond women and their offspring were as disposable as tissue paper, and this image demeaned women. Like the monthly centrefolds in *Playboy*, they were to be looked at, lusted after, and tossed aside. *You Only Live Twice* did little to dispel this notion.

The film opens with Bond in bed with Ling (Tsai Chin), a Chinese woman enlisted to help stage 007's fake murder. By this point, Bond's reputation as an indestructible womanizer virtually required that for people to believe he had been shot dead, his body needed to be found in the bed of an exotic woman.

Sent to Japan, Bond meets Aki (Akiko Wakabayashi), another spy. Aki virtually defines inscrutability. She answers questions in short, cryptic sentences, issues instructions like a schoolteacher, and generally patronizes Bond. When he ends up being chased by guards from a Tokyo office building, Aki mysteriously shows up, rescuing him. Bond reasonably asks, 'What's the score?'

'What do you mean? My job is to help you' Aki responds with mock innocence '... I have no information to give you.' She then leaps from her sports car, runs into an abandoned subway station, and leads Bond to a trapdoor entrance to the office of her boss, Tiger Tanaka, head of the Secret Intelligence Service.

We next meet Aki when she slips into a room in Tanaka's house and replaces a bikini-clad servant giving Bond a massage. Remarkably, Bond and Aki greet each other like long-separated lovers. She declares, 'I think I will enjoy very much serving under you,' as Bond carries her off in his arms.

There is an undeniably funny quality of self-parody to all of this, just as when Tanaka declares that he wants Bond to consider, 'my house yours, including all of my possessions'. The next image is four beautiful Japanese women parading out like chattels in white bikinis to give Bond and Tanaka a bath. Tanaka informs Bond, 'In Japan, men always come first; women come second.' This line was brilliantly parodied in *Austin Powers, International Man of Mystery* (1997) when Austin adds the coda, 'if at all'.

Aki is not only sexual set-dressing. She coolly drives Bond out of Tokyo as they are chased by a carload of villains. She does not cling to Bond when they face gunfire or threats of violence. But there is a forced sense of unearned emotional intimacy. She and Bond are not brought together through a trial by fire or even job-imposed sexual fireworks. There is simply no motivation given for their mutual instant attraction.

During this period, SPECTRE captures James Bond. Helga Brandt, aka SPECTRE Number Eleven (Karin Dor), interrogates Bond, pretends to allow herself to be seduced by him, then tries to kill him in an elaborately staged plane accident. Her plan fails, and she is fed to a pool of piranhas as a result. Although fun to watch, Helga's character is given little to do in comparison with Fiona Volpe in *Thunderball*, the precursor red-headed *femme fatale*.

Aki dies in bed with 007, poisoned in an assassination attempt on his life. She is never mentioned again in the film. She is almost instantly replaced with Kissy (Mie Hama), a character inspired by Kissy Suzuki in Fleming's novel, a pearl-diving *ama* girl cum secret agent. Bond marries her in an attempt to legitimize his cover as a Japanese fisherman.

Kissy and Bond first meet at their faux wedding ceremony. Kissy again gives short, businesslike answers to Bond, providing no initial sexual chemistry. She does casually offer a key clue to the location of SPECTRE's secret rocket base. While climbing up to the lip of the hollowed-out volcano that serves as the villain's lair, Kissy – in the now ubiquitous uniform of a white bikini – asks for a rest. She locks eyes with Bond, and falls into an embrace, a moment interrupted by an enemy helicopter flying past. The pair's only other embrace is at the movie's end, when they are interrupted by M's submarine rising beneath them.

Like Aki, Kissy is an accomplished agent, able to abseil down a cord from the top of the volcano and shoot to kill during the climactic battle (although she spends much of her screen time cowering behind Tiger Tanaka). All in all, Kissy and Aki are nearly identical – and as a result interchangeable. In fact, the two lead actresses did exchange roles shortly before filming began.

Ultimately, all the female characters in *You Only Live Twice* have little impact on the plot. Bond does not save them and they do not make an important choice to save Bond. Nonetheless, the future comrade-in-arms Bond Girls would become some of the most memorable women in the film series.

James Bond prepares to go undercover as a Japanese fisherman. The bath girls on the left are (in no particular order): Mai Ling, Yee-Wah Yang, Yasuko Nagazumi, and Jeanne Roland. Akiko Wakabayashi stands on the right.

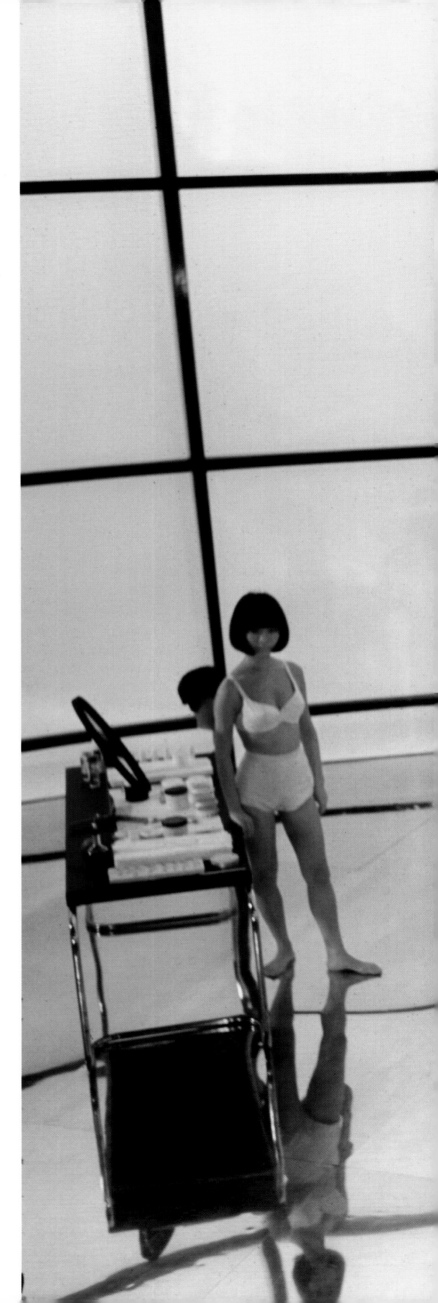

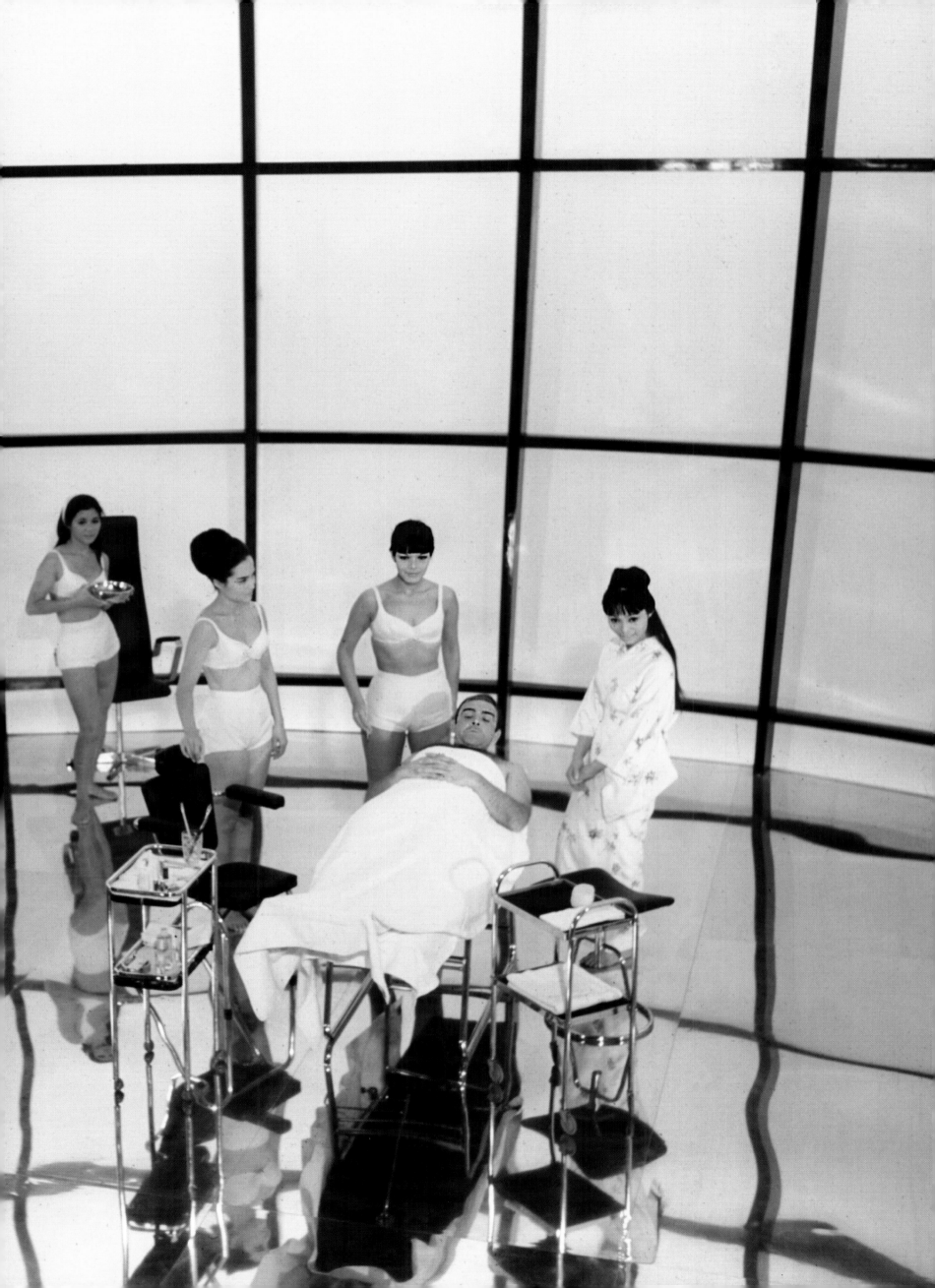

'SHE'S A BIT OF A MIXED UP LADY...AND AT A MOMENT IN HER LIFE WHEN SHE WISHES TO DESTROY EVERYTHING, AND EVERY-THING DOESN'T SEEM WORTHWHILE AT ALL, SHE MEETS AND FALLS IN LOVE WITH JAMES BOND'

DIANA RIGG ON TRACY

On Her Majesty's Secret Service

In 1969, the Bond filmmakers faced the difficult task of introducing a new 007, George Lazenby, in *On Her Majesty's Secret Service*. They also chose to translate one of Fleming's most emotional novels to the screen. They tackled both challenges head on, with a result that has divided critics and fans over the years. Many see *On Her Majesty's Secret Service* as the 'purest' Bond film, the one that feels the most like Ian Fleming's novels. Others have complained that the movie lacks the confident gloss of the earlier and later Bonds. All agree it is not a typical James Bond movie.

In the original 1963 novel (written while *Dr. No* was in production) James Bond falls in love with Comtessa Teresa di Vicenzo (Diana Rigg). Tracy, as she is known, is the emotionally distraught daughter of a notorious crime boss. She has suffered through a love-less marriage and the death of her only child. Like Domino in *Thunderball*, she has a privileged but empty life. 'I gave her too much. It brought her nothing', her father Marc Ange Draco tells Bond in the film. The film omits the death of Tracy's child, but remains true to Fleming's original complex view of her character.

The film opens with Bond rescuing Tracy from an attempted suicide on the Portuguese coast – a stark contrast to the way he meets the vivacious Honey Ryder in *Dr. No*. Later at a casino Tracy commits the self-destructive act of placing a huge bet that she cannot cover. Bond makes good her debt and tells her to 'play it safe' the next time.

'People who want to stay alive play it safe,' she coldly replies.

Nonetheless, Bond makes a pass, and she tosses him her room key, telling him to come later. She, though, is not in her room, but his suite. She manages to take Bond's gun and asks, 'What if I were to kill you for a thrill?'

Compounding Tracy's manic behaviour is the fact that twice Bond has been attacked by anonymous thugs. When Tracy tells Bond that she doesn't know anything about this, he slaps her. She tells him that she may be many things but she is not a liar. This line is delivered with a real sense of pathos, as if honesty and some inner sense of honour is all Tracy has left. She instructs Bond 'to think about me as a woman you've just bought'. Hidden behind her harsh facade is a clearly desperate desire to enjoy one last night of passion before she ends her life.

Draco later tells 007 that the night of passion has been good for Tracy. She apparently hasn't fallen back into a suicidal mood, and Draco believes that she needs a man like Bond in her life. Draco disturbingly adds (backed by a musical sting of 'The James Bond Theme'), 'What she needs is a man to dominate her, to make love to her enough to make her love him.'

The courtship that follows does not reveal much of Bond's relation-ship with Tracy as it occurs under the poignant song, 'We Have All the Time in the World', but by the end, Bond and Tracy are seen eyeing wedding rings. What is clear is that Bond does not 'dominate her' as Draco believes she needs. Bond and Tracy are shown very much as partners.

It is only well after the courtship that the audience sees what potential Bond must have sensed beneath Tracy's troubled behaviour. Tracy rescues Bond in Switzerland, driving and skiing with great skill. Trapped in a barn during a blizzard, Bond proposes marriage. The scene is small, intimate, and playfully real. For some viewers, the moment proved too real, too emotional for the imperturbable secret agent. For others, Bond's profession of love for Tracy made him authentic, complex, and vulnerable. It solidified their view of Bond as more than just a caricature.

Ultimately, Bond and Tracy marry at Draco's estate in Portugal, but any hopes of a happy ending are shattered when Blofeld and his female aide-de-camp, Irma Bunt (Ilse Steppat), murder Tracy with a blast of machine gun fire. Bond cradles Tracy's head in his arms as a patrolman arrives.

'It's all right. It's quite all right really,' Bond tells the officer. 'She's having a rest. We'll be going on soon. There's no hurry you see. We have all the time in the world.' The camera lingers on the lone bullet hole in the windshield of Bond's car as 'The James Bond Theme' coldly kicks in, signalling the shutting of Bond's heart and the return of the dark, sardonic soul of 007.

Tracy is not the only woman in *On Her Majesty's Secret Service*. There are twelve beautiful allergy patients from around the globe undergoing treatment at Blofeld's Swiss clinic. The most well-defined is Ruby Bartlett (Angela Scoular), a young woman from Morecambe Bay, Lancashire, with a desperate medical reaction to chicken. Blofeld not only cures these women, but brainwashes them as well. He refers to them as his angels of death, and they are scheduled to return to their homes across the globe with a bacteriological agent that can devastate crops and livestock, throwing the global economy into turmoil.

While the concept of these characters emanates from Fleming's novel (where they were all British), they stand in stark contrast to Bond's complicated relationship with Tracy. It almost seems as if they are a nod from the filmmakers and Fleming to the audience's desire to see Bond surrounded by more than one beautiful woman, even in a film where he marries the heroine.

Diana Rigg and George Lazenby (opposite) on the casino set in *On Her Majesty's Secret Service*.

Lazenby (below) relaxes at the top of the Schilthorn with Mona Chong and Jenny Hanley.

THE SEVENTIES

I first became aware of James Bond in the Seventies. The films were fantasies and total escapism. I always looked forward to them when I was growing up.

The Seventies were a tumultuous decade for women, who having won some degree of sexual freedom in the Sixties, now demanded freedom of opportunity in the workplace and under the law. The Bond films tried to adapt to the changes going on in society, and they did so by turning to humour with varying degrees of success.

At the beginning of *The Spy Who Loved Me*, there is a moment where the head of the KGB sends for his best spy, agent Triple-X (this was before Vin Diesel was old enough to go to the movies by himself). The movie cuts to a man making love to a woman when a signal interrupts (a music box playing 'Lara's Theme' from *Dr. Zhivago*). The man gets up from bed with a knowing sigh. Surprise, surprise, the woman is Triple-X. The entire joke relies on a sexist expectation that the KGB's best would naturally be a man. This notion seems awkward today, but not in 1977.

Having created those strong, intriguing characters in the Sixties, the filmmakers were not quite sure what to do with them in the Seventies. Today, the female characters of the Seventies Bond films, more than the women from other decades, seem overshadowed by the spectacle.

The Bond Girls of the Seventies shine within their decade. I loved the sassy yet flirtatious wit of Tiffany Case in *Diamonds Are Forever*. A woman can't help but smile when Anya Amasova calmly bests James Bond as they try to figure out clues hidden within a microfilm image during *The Spy Who Loved Me*. It is hard not to take pleasure in seeing Dr Holly Goodhead strap 007 into a centrifuge in *Moonraker*, even though the audience knows that Bond's joyride is certain to go horribly wrong.

Looking back on the Bond films of the decade, even James Bond could not cope with the speed at which the role of women in society was changing.

Maryam d'Abo

Barbara Bach appeared in a few movies in Italy before coming to the attention of the Bond filmmakers.

BY 1970, THE WORLD was a very different place than it had been when *Dr. No* arrived on the scene. In the early and mid-Sixties, the most popular women outside the realm of showbusiness were the English model Jean Shrimpton and Jacqueline Kennedy. With the new decade, a new generation of women were looking towards feminist authors like Germaine Greer and Gloria Steinem. As author Linda Grant noted in her book *Sexing the Millennium*, many felt that the sexual revolution of the Sixties gave women the right to say yes, while feminism gave them the power to say no.

Sean Connery with Jill St John (above) and Lana Wood (opposite) in *Diamonds Are Forever*.

Diamonds Are Forever

Sean Connery returned as James Bond in 1971's *Diamonds Are Forever*, and the world was waiting. After the more emotionally vulnerable Bond in *On Her Majesty's Secret Service*, the first film of the Seventies signalled an attempt to return to the more successful elements of the series, and the filmmakers put an emphasis on a lighter touch.

Diamonds also signalled an adjustment in the way women were portrayed in the Bond films. The characters became stronger in some ways – most of the Bond Girls from this period are more self-confident, stable and independent than the Bond Girls of the Sixties. They are also less serious and less complex.

In *Diamonds Are Forever*, this shift in the role of women meant that the highly emotional relationship between smuggler Tiffany Case and James Bond in the novel was significantly altered for the film. In the movie, Tiffany (Jill St John) is a supremely self-interested character whose main goal is to get as much from a 50,000 carat packet of smuggled diamonds as she can, and when that becomes impossible, she works with Bond to stay out of jail.

Tiffany initially has little use for Bond's come-ons, declaring she never mixes business and pleasure. Her brusque manner is straight from the novel, but on film it is reminiscent of Pussy Galore from *Goldfinger*, Tiffany's closest cinematic counterpart. It is only when Tiffany finds the dead body of a Las Vegas good-time girl in her pool that she begins to realize that something much larger is at play. The body belongs to Plenty O'Toole (Lana Wood) who earlier attached herself to James Bond at a casino, impressed, primarily it seems, by his winnings.

Bond and Tiffany form an uneasy alliance until Tiffany is kidnapped by Blofeld. Bond ultimately finds her clad in a bikini and heels on Blofeld's oil rig cum satellite control base. She attempts to help Bond, but her character lapses into pure comic relief. She switches the wrong satellite control tapes, and while ineptly trying to fire a machine gun, she manages to blast herself into the ocean. Later, when returning with Bond to Britain on an ocean liner, she shows little initiative in the fight scene with thugs Wint and Kidd.

While Tiffany lacks physical skills, the same cannot be said of Bambi (Lola Larson) and Thumper (Trina Parks), the two female guards Bond encounters trying to rescue billionaire Willard Whyte. They become the first women to get the better of Bond in a physical match, at least until he gets them in a pool.

The women of *Diamonds Are Forever* compensate for what they lack in depth with a confident gloss. They give the film an elegant feel with sparkling dialogue and an almost choreographed sense of physical grace. Tiffany and Plenty use their sex appeal simply for financial gain. They are so transparent and comfortable with these motivations that they can hardly be disliked or distrusted for their larcenous hearts. When Bond demands answers from Tiffany and slaps her with his tie, the moment feels unduly harsh. Nothing in the film seems to warrant that kind of violence, and this is largely because of the charm of its very engaging female characters.

Jill St John takes a break on the
set of *Diamonds Are Forever*.

'I BELIEVE THE BOND FILMS ARE THE FIRST PLACE WHERE WOMEN GOT A CHANCE TO BE IN ACTION ROLES'

GLORIA HENDRY (ROSIE CARVER IN *LIVE AND LET DIE*)

Live And Let Die

The same other-worldly dreamlike tone of *Diamonds Are Forever* permeates Roger Moore's first outing as James Bond in *Live and Let Die*. Despite outcries from organizations supporting women's rights, films of the era seemed to be filled with images of violence against women. Moore's first Bond film, in contrast, continued the turn away from realism and created an escapist fantasy with violence that was not particularly violent, sex that was not particularly sexual, and women who were not particularly real. In the James Bond universe, this recipe proved to be highly entertaining.

Roger Moore's Bond is introduced in bed with an Italian spy, Miss Caruso (Madeline Smith). She is unceremoniously shoved into a closet when M and Moneypenny arrive to give Bond his assignment. The scene signalled a greater emphasis on sex comedy in the Roger Moore Bond films of the Seventies.

Live And Let Die featured the first major part for a black woman in a Bond film, Rosie Carver (Gloria Hendry). While two women of colour had appeared in *On Her Majesty's Secret Service* and *Diamonds Are Forever* respectively, Rosie was the first given an instrumental role in the plot. Rosie's assignment from the villain, Dr Kananga, is to lure Bond into a trap, but a tarot card delivered to Bond tips him off that Rosie is a double agent. Nonetheless, there is nothing cold-blooded about Rosie. Even after Bond suspects her deceit, he makes love to her in the jungles of the fictional island of San Monique, then threatens to kill her if she does not tell all.

'But you couldn't. You wouldn't. Not after what we've just done,' Rosie pleads with a smile.

'I certainly wouldn't have killed you before,' Bond calmly replies.

Rosie is killed not by Bond, but by one of Kananga's remote-controlled guns.

Bond's use of sex to get closer to the villain continues later with the heroine, Solitaire (Jane Seymour). She is a virgin, a fortune-teller who predicts the future for Dr Kananga with tarot cards. Her first meeting with Bond differs from the novel in that she seems very comfortable in her position in Kananga's organization. After Kananga's alter-ego, Mr Big, orders Bond killed, Solitaire allows 007 to select one last card. It is, ominously, the Lovers. As Bond is dragged into a back alley to be shot, he blithely comments that he 'shan't be long'. The impact on Solitaire is more profound. She believes in the cards, and Bond's selection of the Lovers is a sign of fate.

Bond later conducts one of the most amusingly mercenary seductions in the film series. He asks her, 'But you do believe? I mean really believe in the cards?'

'They have never lied to me,' Solitaire replies.

'Then they won't now. Pick one.' Bond fans out a tarot deck and Solitaire selects. The card is, of course, the Lovers. Bond has taken no chances. He drops the deck as they embrace, revealing that the cards are all Lovers. Thus proceeds the first and only virgin deflowering of the Bond film series. Bond's comeuppance for abusing Solitaire's belief system is that, to his dismay, Solitaire can no longer see the future.

Solitaire has none of Bond's trademark coolness under pressure. That said, her supposed powers carry more weight in the film as they represent the one avenue for Bond to attack Kananga and hurt the villain personally.

On another level, her character has an interesting journey. She begins steeped in superstition, only to become someone who embraces the more temporal pleasures of James Bond's world. In the end, she is gleefully playing gin rummy rather than turning tarot cards. She has ceased to dabble in the murky undefined world of the future and has chosen to live for the moment.

'MISS ANDERS... I DIDN'T RECOGNIZE YOU WITH YOUR CLOTHES ON'

BOND TO ANDREA ANDERS (MAUD ADAMS)

IN *THE MAN WITH THE GOLDEN GUN*

The Man With The Golden Gun

In *The Man With The Golden Gun* the filmmakers chose to move even further in the direction of Feydeau farce, poking fun at the sexual misadventures of 007. This element tended to weaken the female characters in the film, particularly Andrea Anders (Maud Adams), the character who puts the story in motion.

Andrea, who has no counterpart in Fleming's posthumously published 1965 novel, is the kept woman of Francisco Scaramanga, aka 'the man with the golden gun'. Scaramanga is a million-dollar-a-shot hitman, working to take control of a new profitable solar energy technology. To escape Scaramanga's clutches, Andrea sends one of Scaramanga's prized golden bullets to Her Majesty's Secret Service inscribed with Bond's number. Bond confronts Andrea in Hong Kong's Peninsula Hotel and proceeds to rough her up trying to get information from her. It is an uncomfortable scene in which Bond seems disturbingly violent. At this point Andrea curiously does not reveal her part in sending the bullet to Bond, so he naturally assumes she is a potential enemy.

In contrast to the serious and tragic figure of Andrea, Bond is accompanied on his mission by his Hong Kong aide-de-camp, Mary Goodnight (Britt Ekland). Bond and Goodnight have known each other from her time with the Secret Service in London. Sadly, despite an engaging personality, Mary is played for laughs. Bond's seduction is presented as hopelessly obvious. Goodnight plays along for a while only to relish her enjoyment of rebuking Bond. Nonetheless, she appears in Bond's suite ready for a night of passion only moments later.

Before Bond can bed Goodnight, Andrea shows up. Bond bundles Goodnight under the bedclothes and later shoves her into a closet while he convinces Andrea to give him the invaluable Solex agitator device held by Scaramanga. Andrea pleads with Bond to kill Scaramanga, even offering herself as an inducement. Thus, with Goodnight crammed in a hiding place, Bond makes love to Andrea. He even leaves Goodnight inside long enough for Andrea to return to Scaramanga's junk. Awakening Goodnight, Bond condescendingly apologizes, 'Forgive me darling, but your turn will come. I promise.'

Goodnight's character seems like an appendage – a loyal, lovesick, and somewhat incompetent assistant who does not really fit into the James Bond universe. Andrea is also somewhat roughly drawn, but far more compelling in her potential. Sadly, Scaramanga kills Andrea, and Goodnight becomes the film's bumbling heroine, inevitably finding herself in situations such as being locked in the boot of Scaramanga's car. She ends the film wandering on Scaramanga's island in a bikini, blithely causing problems such as setting off a chain reaction that blows the island to bits. Needless to say, Bond finds this exasperating, but left without an alternative, he happily takes her in his arms at the film's end. Goodnight's turn finally comes.

There are two competent and dangerous girls in the film – schoolgirl nieces of Bond's ally, Lieutenant Hip. Played by Joie Vejjijiva and Cheung Chuen Nam, the schoolgirls rescue Bond from a small army of karate students, comically chopping their way through Bond's assailants. They are portrayed in a way that mocks their skill rather than celebrates it.

Looking back on the films of the period, current Bond producer Barbara Broccoli, who was herself a teenager in the Seventies, comments, 'Personally, I think in the Seventies, the women in the Bond films reflected the more materialistic values of that decade.'

The filmmakers wanted to find the proper balance between the humour the films needed and strong roles for the leading females. In the next film in the series, they would concentrate on this problem, creating an engaging female spy forced to work with Bond.

'WHEN THIS MISSION IS OVER I WILL KILL YOU'

ANYA IN *THE SPY WHO LOVED ME*

The Spy Who Loved Me

After *The Man With The Golden Gun*, producer Harry Saltzman sold his share of 007, leaving Cubby Broccoli in charge of the series. It was a period of détente between the Soviet Union and the West, and it was also a period where the core idea of equal opportunity for women was finally taking hold, with the Equal Pay Bill coming into force in 1975. The concept of 'equal pay for equal work' was the inspiration behind the character of Soviet KGB Major Anya Amasova, aka Triple X (Barbara Bach). What if Bond were confronted with his equal in every respect, and she was a woman?

Aside from working for different sides on a joint mission, Major Amasova and Commander Bond have another, darker connection that the audience knows but the characters for most of the film do not. During the film's opening, Bond murdered Amasova's lover in self-defence. Thus there is a nice bit of tension for the audience as viewers await this revelation and its ramifications. When Anya does discover Bond's involvement, she declares, 'When this mission is over, I will kill you.'

In the end, Bond slays the proverbial dragon and rescues Anya from the villain's clutches. Anya tries to muster her conviction that she should still kill Bond, but she can't. His killing of her former lover was not personal, but his effort to save her was.

While Anya does end up as a 'damsel in distress', she is a strong, equal, and interesting character in a very glossy film. She is also one of the best comrade-in-arms characters in the series because even until the very end, there is a wonderful tension between her and 007.

The Spy Who Loved Me contains numerous other Bond Girls in lesser parts. There is the Soviet agent bedding Bond on a bearskin rug at the beginning of the film (Sue Vanner), a woman killed in Bond's arms (Felicca, played by Olga Bisera) as he searches for information on disappearing submarines, and Naomi (Caroline Munro), a wonderfully sexy *femme fatale* who tries to kill Bond and Anya in a helicopter assault. Almost as if to balance the strong characters of Anya and Naomi, there is also a throwaway harem from which Bond is invited to choose a partner for the night.

Bond (Roger Moore) finds his fate in the hands of Anya (Barbara Bach) at the end of his mission. Director Lewis Gilbert: 'In *The Spy Who Loved Me*, we had, for the first time, a Russian spy going alongside James Bond. They fell in love naturally. That hadn't happened before, really. By and large, the Russians were the enemy.'

Moonraker

Moonraker tried to duplicate the success of *The Spy Who Loved Me*, including pairing Bond with a female secret agent who was every bit as smart and adventurous as 007. The film, though, is very much a comedy that takes the elements of Bond's world purely for granted, and that includes the women. The heroine of the film is Dr Holly Goodhead (Lois Chiles), a Vassar-educated CIA officer working under-cover in the villain's organization, supposedly on loan from NASA. She is fully trained as an astronaut and, overachiever that she is, exhibits a condescending view of James Bond. In fact, Bond often seems to be one step behind Holly in unravelling the mystery of the missing space shuttle. She is just as conniving as Bond when it comes to the merce-nary use of sex. In Venice, she sleeps with Bond to create the illusion that she is willing to pool resources with him. The pair end the film making love in zero gravity aboard a space shuttle.

Like Anya in *The Spy Who Loved Me*, Holly is portrayed throughout the film as Bond's equal. She comports herself well during the fights and never really seems to need Bond's help in any situation, except for a battle on top of the Urca Hill – Sugar Loaf mountain cable cars. Both Holly and Bond have the same goals – stopping the villain Drax. The conflict between Holly and Bond is played for comic relief, as is any legitimate form of sexual attraction.

Bond also has another female comrade-in-arms, Manuela (Emily Bolton) of Station VH in Rio. She may be Bond's fastest seduction – Manuela and Bond have only been in each other's presence for exactly one minute before Bond propositions her. She quietly disap-pears from the film shortly afterwards.

Drax's helicopter pilot, Corinne Dufour (Corinne Clery), also aids 007. Bond offers to sleep with her if she will help uncover informa-tion. Corinne goes for the idea, and the following day, Drax, having discovered her treachery, unleashes his guard dogs on her.

Other beautiful women populate the film – another *femme fatale* with Bond during the film's opening (Leila Shenna) and legions of 'perfect' women for Drax's space-base repopulation scheme. It is all self-parody and sketch comedy on the scale of a Biblical epic. In that environment, the women of *Moonraker* often fare better than Bond.

Lois Chiles on Holly Goodhead: 'I liked Holly, and I liked that she was capable of doing everything that Bond could do. It was a real step forward in the James Bond genre in terms of modernization.'

THE EIGHTIES

If the keynote of the sexual climate during the Seventies was women's liberation, the keynote of the Eighties was AIDS.

During the first half of the decade films seemed to shrink away from sexual tension. After Roger Moore left the role of Bond, the movies had to adapt to the political landscape. Sex was no longer scandalous; it was potentially deadly.

A new crop of Bond Girls was the result of this shift in tone. They were more conservative and in some ways naive, such as Melina Havelock in *For Your Eyes Only*, Stacey Sutton in *A View To A Kill*, and my character, Kara Milovy in *The Living Daylights*. It was a strange time of shifting roles for women. The new icons of the Eighties had to find a balance; Madonna seemed to know how to mix her sexuality with her power, but much of popular culture was rebelling against the morals of the Sixties.

In the US, then Vice President Dan Quayle spoke about family values. Germaine Greer wrote an influential book, *Sex and Destiny* (1984) about how society undervalued the role of women as mothers. In it, she argued for integrating children into daily life.

The women in the Bond films were right for the times, reflecting ordinary women in extraordinary situations. Melina Havelock was out to avenge the murder of her family. Stacey Sutton sought to protect her family's oil business. Through 007's strange spyglass, family values were alive and well.

This is not to say that the Bond women of the era were demure. They were willing to deceive, seduce and even kill alongside 007. Larger than life characters like Octopussy and May Day (in *A View To A Kill*) kept Bond's adventures fun.

The films underwent a tremendous shift when Roger Moore left the role after 1985's *A View To A Kill*. Timothy Dalton and the filmmakers felt it was time to return to Ian Fleming's original concept of the character of James Bond. Throughout the Eighties, the leading roles for Bond women were more human, more real and less iconic.

By the end of the decade reality was quickly catching up with James Bond. In 1989, shortly after *Licence To Kill* appeared on cinema screens, the Cold War ended. James Bond – or at least the films' producers – went off to fight legal battles that sidelined new Bond movies for six years.

Maryam d'Abo

Maryam d'Abo: 'For my role as Kara in *The Living Daylights*, I had to learn how to play the cello without making any sound, otherwise I would have driven everyone crazy. The secret? We used soap on the bow.'

IF A DISTANT CIVILIZATION could only judge our society by the films of the early Eighties, they might be forgiven for thinking that a woman's right of passage was running from crazed men and monsters armed with large sharp objects. Starting with *Halloween* (1978), the slasher genre quickly took the heat of feminists' ire off the Bond films. While critics decried the new turn of explicit and often sexual violence portrayed in these films, the Bond filmmakers made a move away from comedy, and sought to create female characters more in the Fleming mould.

For Your Eyes Only

After the excess of *Moonraker*, the filmmakers decided to return Bond to his Fleming roots. Working with the stories 'For Your Eyes Only', 'Risico' and unused scenes from the novels *Live And Let Die* and *Goldfinger*, Michael G. Wilson (stepson of producer Cubby Broccoli) partnered with long-time Bond screenwriter Richard Maibaum. The pair fashioned a script with a story similar to *From Russia With Love* (Britain and the Soviet Union vying for a piece of intelligence technology) and a heroine who harked back to Bond's literary roots.

The film opens with Bond standing at the grave of his short-lived wife, Tracy, a reference not only to Bond's past, but a sign that the women of this film may be taken more seriously than the outings of the Seventies.

The central heroine of the film, Melina Havelock (Carole Bouquet), is based heavily on Judy Havelock from the short story 'For Your Eyes Only'. Melina's parents are engaged in a deep sea recovery operation for British intelligence until a Cuban hitman murders the couple before Melina's eyes. Melina's desire for vengeance against those involved in crime is played for real. She is drawn into the dark underside of international politics by pain and anger, and she wants a grave wrong set right. Bond attempts to convince her that she must be prepared for the consequences of revenge: 'First, dig two graves,' he says, quoting a Chinese proverb. Melina prefers Greek mythology, citing Electra's desire to avenge her father's death. Melina fails to note that Electra is miserable and consumed by guilt

in the classic drama by Euripides.

On one side, Melina represents the hot-blooded desire for retribution and vengeance. She is eager to kill anyone she finds connected to the crime. On the other, Bond is a more detached killer. Bond's discussions with Melina on the subject of revenge are sometimes patronizing in tone, but they do form the moral basis of the film's central question – how to achieve justice in an unjust world? In some ways it feels as if Melina makes Bond a more moral and careful secret agent in the story, just as Bond tempers Melina from letting her anger rule her actions.

Melina has skills that complement Bond's – expertise with a crossbow, knowledge of and access to deep sea diving equipment. Ultimately, they share adventures that bring them closer emotionally, although in the end Melina still wants revenge against Kristatos, the man who ordered the murder of her parents. Kristatos is killed, but not in cold blood, and not by Melina.

Two other women play a part in the film. First, Bond meets a young skater named Bibi Dahl (Lynn-Holly Johnson), whom Kristatos sponsors and hopes will be an Olympic champion. Despite Bibi's innocent exterior, she eagerly throws herself into Bond's bed. For once, Bond objects, feeling she is entirely too young. Bond does not object to the advances of Countess Lisl Von Schlaf (Cassandra Harris), a woman actually from Liverpool, who is used by Bond's future ally Columbo to seduce him into a trap. She dies at the hand of one of Kristatos's henchmen.

Carole Bouquet (opposite and above with Roger Moore) was a successful model and actress at age twenty. She appeared in Luis Buñuel's 1977 classic, *That Obscure Object of Desire*, before linking with 007 at the age of twenty-four.

Octopussy

Octopussy is a lavish entry into the Bond series. Made during the same period as the non-EON Bond movie, *Never Say Never Again*, it features much of the realism of *For Your Eyes Only* with a more fantastic plot and a conscious effort to include ingredients familiar to the loyal James Bond audience.

The movie features two strong female roles, both enigmatic and both reminiscent of Edwardian adventure fiction. The first is Magda (Kristina Wayborn), a mysterious woman apparently in league with one of the villains, smuggler and Afghan Prince Kamal Kahn. She happily seduces Bond to retrieve a Fabergé egg that he 'acquired' from a London auction. As cover, she works for Octopussy's circus as a close-up magician. Unlike many Bond women, her decision to work with Bond in the film's finale is not based on an emotional or sexual connection.

Octopussy (Maud Adams) is Magda's boss. It turns out that Bond confronted Octopussy's father, Major Dexter Smythe, with evidence implicating him in a murder years earlier. For some reason, Octopussy, now one of the world's pre-eminent smugglers, wants to thank Bond for allowing her father the 'honourable' way out – suicide rather than the disgrace of a court martial. It is her father, an expert on octopi, who burdened her with the nickname 'Octopussy'. She now runs an all-female gang similar to Pussy Galore's Flying Circus (*Goldfinger*), except that Octopussy's circus is earthbound. She believes her crimes consist solely of smuggling Kremlin jewels to the West. In fact, she is a pawn in a far more sinister plot.

Octopussy claims that she and Bond are 'two of a kind'. She even tries to induce Bond to join her organization. Ultimately she must risk her organization and her future when Bond, in clown make-up, tells her there is a nuclear bomb in one of the circus props, and there are only seconds to go before detonation.

After the bomb is defused, Octopussy helps track down the true villain, Kamal Khan, who betrayed her. She and her gang work with Bond to destroy Kamal's operation.

Octopussy strikes a fine balance between audacious sexiness and strong female characters. The title itself dictates a certain tone. The film successfully embodies a sense of feminine empowerment that was attractive to both men and women. Octopussy's fetching female gang often manage to wear as little as possible. That given, they are not only pleasing to the eye, but accomplished, confident women. Each is a circus performer, oarsman, smuggler, and trained commando. The final assault on Kamal's palace is a bit of ludicrous but enjoyable fantasy, with a corps of fighting women in black leather bikinis who deftly manage to overcome the better-armed guards. Bond's damsel-in-distress rescue of Octopussy at the end does not undercut her strength or the drama of her earlier choice to side with him.

Maud Adams on Octopussy: 'I loved this character because she was so opposite to Andrea [in *The Man With The Golden Gun*]. She runs this international smuggling operation, she has all these women working for her, and she's a fun, exciting character.'

'I THOUGHT THAT CREEP LOVED ME'

MAY DAY IN *A VIEW TO A KILL*

Never Say Never Again

This film grew out of many legal battles between Bond producer Cubby Broccoli and Kevin McClory over the screen rights to the novel *Thunderball* and various screenplays developed before and after its publication. Thus, the film exists, like *Casino Royale*, outside EON Productions' series. It also marked the brief return of Sean Connery to the role of Bond.

The women who appear in *Never Say Never Again* are almost all reincarnations of more interestingly drawn characters from *Thunderball*. The most impressive is Fatima Blush (Barbara Carrera) renamed from Fiona Volpe (played by Luciana Paluzzi) in the earlier film. Her over-the-top love of sex and death rarely fails to amuse the most jaded viewers. Aside from Domino (Kim Basinger) and Patricia (Prunella Gee), 007 also beds a woman (Valerie Leon) he finds on a fishing boat but who has nothing to do with his mission.

Grace Jones told US television host Johnny Carson in 1985 that she enjoyed working with Roger Moore. 'I tell you, I think all we thought about before the love scene was the love scene ... it was great. He has such a funny sense of humour.'

A View To A Kill

A View To A Kill appeared just as the action hero film craze of the Eighties was getting into full swing. Those films, best represented by movies such as *First Blood* (1982) and its sequel *Rambo: First Blood Part II* (1987), *Terminator* (1984), *Robocop* (1987) and *Die Hard* (1988) offered similar stunts and over-the-top villains to Bond but generally lacked any meaningful roles for women, and very little in the way of sex appeal. In contrast, 1985's *A View To A Kill* starred many beautiful women and was full of sexual innuendo.

First is May Day (Grace Jones), a delightfully over-the-top *femme fatale*. Although she converts to Bond's side at the very end, she only does so because master villain Max Zorin attempts to kill her, not because of Bond's skill as a seducer. Bond also encounters two fellow spies, although the first (Mary Stavin) appears for mere moments in a submarine disguised as an iceberg. The second is KGB agent Pola Ivanova (Fiona Fullerton), who is also after Zorin. She is a former ballet dancer once sent to seduce Bond. She playfully consorts with 007 in a San Francisco hot tub, then disappears after he steals a tape she has made of Zorin's private conversations.

The central heroine of the film is Stacey Sutton (Tanya Roberts), an oil heiress cheated by Zorin out of her share of her family's company. Now a geologist for the State of California's Department of Conservation, she is battling to regain control of the family fortune. Stacey has a strong understanding of fault lines and geology, but her emotional fragility and lack of physical confidence in the rough and tumble world of Bond weakens her character. Ultimately she is in need more of Bond's protection than his attention. Stacey represents the approach to the leading women taken in three of the Bond films of the Eighties. She is an ordinary woman in extraordinary circumstances. While neither she nor Melina in *For Your Eyes Only* has the exotic aura of Pussy Galore or Honey Ryder, they are more real and their goals are fuelled by personal conflicts with the villains. These qualities would be especially true of the heroine in the next Bond film.

The Living Daylights

The year 1987 marked the twenty-fifth anniversary of the Bond films. For the filmmakers the anniversary posed a double challenge. Not only did they need to introduce a new James Bond in the form of Timothy Dalton, but they also needed to confront a growing crisis. Since the early Eighties, the spectre of AIDS/HIV had brought serious reconsideration of the more casual aspects of the sexual revolution. By 1986, health professionals urged restraint and responsibility in the media in the depiction of sex.

In *The Living Daylights*, for the first time, it is not clear whether or not Bond ever sleeps with any of the women he meets on his mission; the final embrace with Kara Milovy (Maryam d'Abo) strongly implies that more will follow between them, but in every other film, Bond has at least one liaison during the course of the story. Bond first meets a woman (Kell Tyler) on a yacht who offers him champagne, but he never even kisses her on-screen. Later, Bond is drawn into a complex relationship with Kara, a Czech cellist deeply in love with one of the film's central villains, Soviet General Georgi Koskov. Kara even helps Koskov stage his defection to the West early in the film, posing as a KGB assassin.

Kara, like Octopussy and Pussy Galore (*Goldfinger*), does not realize that the villain is using her. Rather than openly seduce Kara, Bond gains her trust by claiming to be a friend of Koskov's. Their shared adventures, particularly escaping from Czechoslovakia to Austria and a night in Vienna's famed Prater amusement park, help build emotional closeness.

As in *A View To A Kill*, Bond is more paternal than a partner. His continued deception of Kara undercuts her trust. Traditionally, the characters like Kara who are under the control of the villain (like Tatiana, Domino and Solitaire) must make a choice to stay with the villain or take the more risky path and side with Bond. In *The Living Daylights*, Kara, still under the illusion that Koskov loves her, chooses him over Bond. She serves Bond a drugged drink and only later realizes that Koskov has no further use for her.

Kara's musical skills — she is a world-class concert performer — show her to be an elegant and accomplished woman. While not an espionage agent, she has a ready willingness to face any adventure, and she handles a horse like a pro. Once she decides to link herself to Bond, she quickly develops a mad crush. It is hard to know if Bond shares her attraction. Early on, Bond is peeved about having to rescue her prized cello (a Stradivarius named The Lady Rose). He later seems irritated that she cannot easily read his hand signals instructing her to drive a Jeep into a taxiing military cargo plane.

Kara's great moment comes when Bond is trapped on a truck headed into a Soviet military base in Afghanistan. Kara turns to a group of mujahedin warriors and insists that they risk their lives to save Bond. They balk at openly attacking the vastly superior Soviet forces, but Kara pulls a rifle from the saddle of the leader, Kamran Shah, and rides off in disgust to save Bond alone. Kamran Shah and his men, shamed by Kara's courage, can do nothing but follow.

Maryam d'Abo: 'Michael Wilson took this photo at Ouarzazate, Morocco. I loved this location. It was so new to me to be in the desert — exciting and inspiring. The dawns and sunsets were just mind-blowing.'

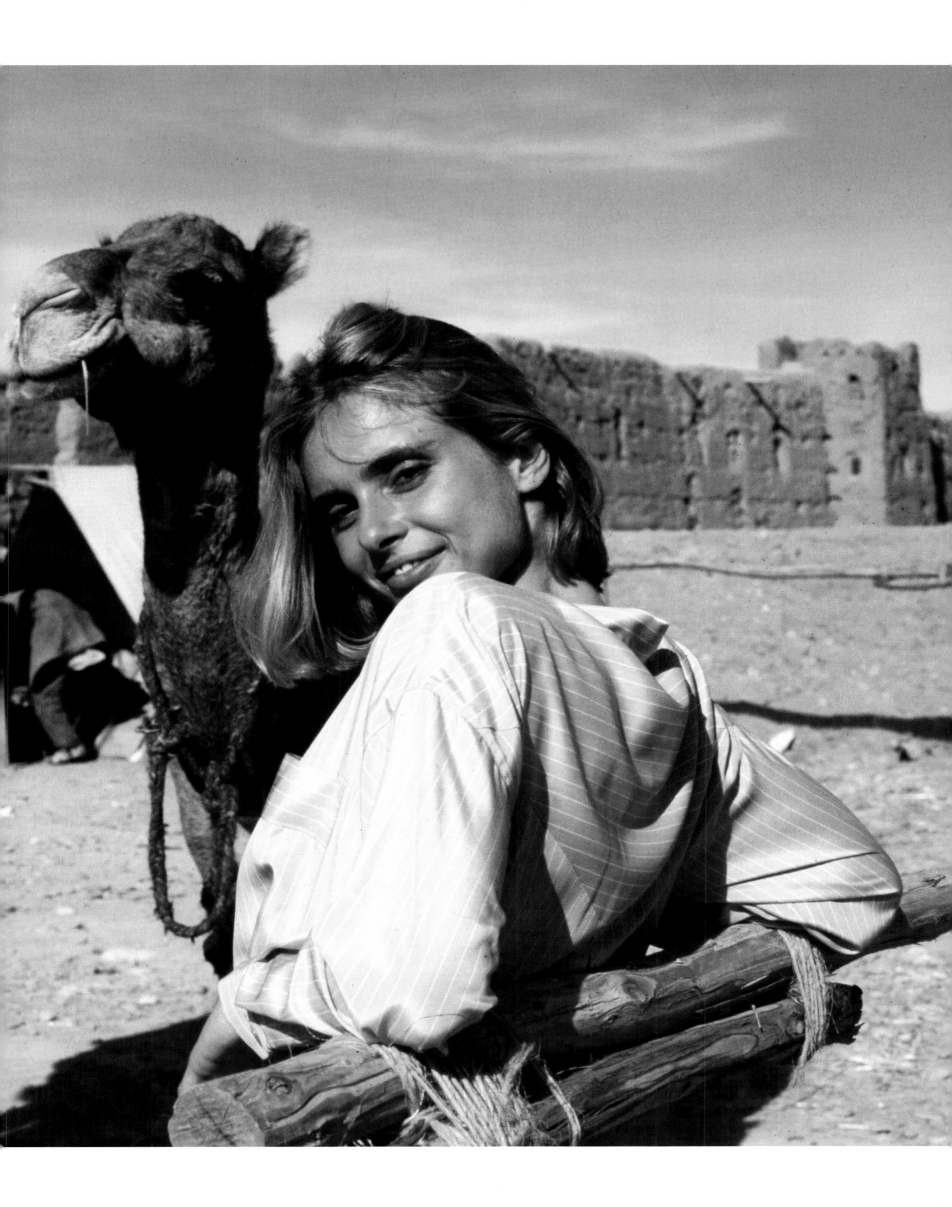

Talisa Soto (above) recalls how the character of Lupe changed during shooting. 'She was truly a villain at first, but as we were working there were rewrites. They decided to soften her up and make her fall in love with James Bond.'

Carey Lowell (opposite) on how she approached the role of Pam Bouvier: 'I basically just tried to relax because it was such a huge pair of shoes to fill, to come in and be a Bond Girl.'

Licence To Kill

Licence To Kill in 1989 offered a darker view of Bond and two strong competing Bond Girls. The first is Lupe Lamora (Talisa Soto), the tormented lover of drug lord Franz Sanchez. The second is a former US Army and CIA pilot, Pam Bouvier (Carey Lowell), who is an informant for the Drug Enforcement Agency. This film, though, heralded a new era of 007. The women in Bond's life throughout the Nineties would generally be stronger and more self-assured. Pam Bouvier paved the road for those characters to come.

Pam has a CV more impressive than some members of the US Joint Chiefs of Staff, complemented by tremendous fighting skills. She is unimpressed by Bond's Walther PPK when the pair confront Sanchez's men in a bar in Bimini, instead preferring a short-barrel shotgun. Perhaps as with Holly Goodhead in *Moonraker*, Bond seems overwhelmed by this woman's confidence and strength. However, Pam has more in common with Bond. Like him, danger only seems to excite her. Shortly after being shot in the back – and saved by a Kevlar vest – she makes a pass at Bond, wiping away the blood from the corner of his mouth before kissing him. 'Why don't you wait until you're asked?' Bond wants to know.

'Why don't you ask me?' Pam responds.

In fact, neither of these two ever do much asking. They issue orders to each other throughout the film. In the fictional country of Isthmus, Bond gains the upper hand in two ways. First, as he informs Pam, 'We're south of the border. It's a man's world.' He forces her to pose as his executive secretary, Ms Kennedy (a clever alias as Bouvier was former First Lady Jacqueline Kennedy's maiden name). Secondly, Bond, by sleeping with Lupe, sends the otherwise steel-nerved Ms Bouvier into a bit of an emotional tailspin. 'I'll be damned if I help him!' she proclaims after Lupe reveals her night of passion with Bond.

Considering Bond's previous relationships with women – especially with those who are emotionally wounded like Tracy in *On Her Majesty's Secret Service* – fans might have thought Lupe, who is beaten by Sanchez for infidelity earlier in the film, would warrant Bond's ultimate affection. Instead, when Lupe invites Bond to stay with her in Isthmus, Bond understands her mercenary survival skills are not for him, at least not for more than the one night they spent together. He chooses Pam.

THE NINETIES
AND BEYOND

When the filmmakers prepared to make *GoldenEye* in 1995, they faced an interesting question. How should they refer to the women in the James Bond films? The term 'Bond Girls' seemed to denote immature playmates, female characters who existed merely for 007's pleasure. As the term 'politically correct' worked its way into everyday language, the decision was clear – in the Nineties, there would be no 'Bond Girls', only 'Bond Women'.

Women became a key part of James Bond's successful return as a pop culture icon. Barbara Broccoli became the first female producer on the Bond films, but she was not a lone female voice in a male-dominated world. As producer Michael Wilson told me during the production of *Die Another Day*, 'Half of my executives are women. My mother is the chairman of the company. Our chief financial officer is a woman and our chief publicity officer is a woman. We also have a lot of input from women in our scripts.'

On the literary side, Ian Fleming's nieces – Kate Grimmond and Lucy Fleming – became more involved in the management of the 007 novels. Former Penguin editor Kate Jones spearheaded the publication of the successful fiftieth anniversary editions of the original James Bond stories.

What was the impact of a healthy dose of oestrogen on James Bond? The character, as played by Pierce Brosnan, understood innately the strengths and talents of his counterparts. The old masculine assumptions about a woman's limitations totally disappeared in the Nineties, including the appointment of a woman as head of British Intelligence, MI5.

As the Nineties progressed, women became more and more comfortable with expressing their sexuality without any of the defensiveness that seemed so prevalent in the Eighties. With films like the Bond-inspired Austin Powers movies celebrating the exuberant Sixties view of sex, young women began openly embracing characters like Honey Ryder and Pussy Galore.

The Bond women of the Nineties – like Xenia Onatopp, Wai Lin and Elektra King – captured the playful sensuality of the Sixties while maintaining the dramatic complexity viewers expect in films today. These characters were strong, independent, and bowed to no one. Their sex appeal was only part of their power. By the turn of the millennium London boutiques sold T-shirts to young women with the words 'Bond Babe' across the front.

By the time production began on *Die Another Day*, actress Rosamund Pike showed no doubts about defining her character with the term reviled by feminists in the Seventies and Eighties. 'I don't want to be called a Bond Woman. I think Bond Girl is sexier.' The tide had turned. The new generation of actresses happily adopt the Bond Girl image, not because it excites men or is expected by some male-driven film publicity machine, but because it represents this generation's own fantasies and aspirations of confidence, beauty, and clout. As Pike told me, 'When someone says, "What are you doing?" and you say, "I'm the new Bond Girl," their face just lights up. It's an immensely powerful thing.'

Power comes from respect, and by the new millennium the Bond Girls – having survived the sexual revolution, the battle for women's rights, the changing tastes and morality of the past forty years – had earned the respect of men and women around the world.

Maryam d'Abo

Co-writer Neal Purvis on Jinx (Halle Berry): 'She is effectively someone who lives in the shadow of death all the time and therefore takes her pleasure where she can. And in that respect Jinx is much like Bond.'

Izabella Scorupco (opposite and above with Pierce Brosnan) on Natalya Simonova: 'She knows the rules. She's a Russian, even if it's not the Communist government any more, she's still very careful and nervous.'

SIX AND A HALF YEARS would pass between the release of *Licence To Kill* and James Bond's return to cinemas. The length of time could not measure the global changes that took place in 007's absence. James Bond sat out the end of the Cold War, which transformed the geopolitical landscape that gave birth to 007. The continued success of nearly sexless large-scale action films like *Terminator 2: Judgement Day* (1991), *Cliffhanger* (1993), and *True Lies* (1994) altered the way audiences viewed action-adventure films. To many Hollywood observers these films rendered James Bond outdated. As challenging for the filmmakers, the notion of a hero moving from film to film and heroine to heroine seemed out of sync with the movies of the era. The heroines of *Thelma and Louise* (1991) had driven off a cliff rather than subject themselves to an abusive world ruled by men. Would movie-goers accept Bond Girls in the politically correct world of the Nineties?

The answer was a resounding 'yes'. The producers, now Michael Wilson and Barbara Broccoli, not only cast Pierce Brosnan as James Bond, but also focused on the role of 'the Bond woman', deciding to keep the sexual adventurism from Bond's past successes, but to make an extra effort to bring dimension to the female characters.

GoldenEye

GoldenEye featured three Bond women. The first, is a brief appearance by Caroline (Serena Gordon), a psychiatrist working for MI6 sent to evaluate Bond in Monte Carlo. She is a comic figure, who is finally seduced by everything that intellectually she finds so abhorrent in Bond – his womanizing, his love of danger, his enthusiasm for sports cars and expensive champagne. She is a vehicle for the audience to, in a way, accept that Bond is not your typical Nineties man; he is his own man, and a very desirable man at that.

In the very same scene Bond notices Xenia Onatopp (Famke Janssen), an ex-Soviet fighter pilot working with the Russian-based Janus crime syndicate. Xenia is the villain Trevelyan's henchman, for lack of a better term, a *femme fatale* whose preferred method of killing is crushing men with her thighs (in *The Living Daylights* there is mention of a hefty female KGB assassin who uses this technique).

Xenia is the spiritual kin of Fiona Volpe (*Thunderball*), except that she enjoys her work just a little too much. Her sexual stimulation as she guns down workers at a satellite control station is a bit creepy, but her gasps of pleasure as she chokes the life out of a Navy admiral reveal a starkly twisted mind. One thing is for certain – she is captivating to watch, laying bare all the unspoken darkness of the traditional *femme fatale*. She is ultimately crushed herself, yanked by a climbing rope attached to a helicopter into the 'thighs' of a forking tree trunk.

As if to compensate for the over-the-top Onatopp, Natalya Simonova (Izabella Scorupco) has a humdrum life before tragedy strikes her world. Onatopp murders all her co-workers in an attempt to take over Russia's two satellite weapons. In many ways, Natalya is similar to Kara Milovy in *The Living Daylights*. She has a misguided emotional attachment to one of the villains – a computer programmer who she does not realize is part of the deadly plot. She is left for dead, and when the villain finds out she is alive, like Kara, she is lured into a trap.

On the other hand, Natalya spends almost all of the second half of the film as an equal of Bond's whose skills and knowledge are vital to the success of the mission. Unlike Kara, Natalya has nothing left to lose when she meets 007, nor does she have anything to gain by preserving the status quo. Her relationship with him does not put her at greater risk. She is a strong, forceful character. She even hijacks an enemy helicopter to help save Bond from a collapsing satellite transmitter.

Natalya's courage and confidence in the action scenes appear to come from her own inner reservoir, and not out of her interaction with Bond. She is a born survivor drawn into a plot where those skills come to the fore. She proves to be a worthy trendsetter for the Nineties Bond Girls.

Tomorrow Never Dies

The success of *GoldenEye* in reintroducing James Bond to film audiences allowed for a confident swagger evident in 1997's *Tomorrow Never Dies*. Aside from a Dutch professor named Inga Bergstrom (Cecilie Thomsen) whom Bond beds early in the movie, he encounters two significant women in the course of his adventure. The first is Paris (Teri Hatcher) a former lover who has made the mistake of marrying a megalomaniac press baron named Elliot Carver. Bond abandoned Paris (now Mrs Carver) years ago, and she has obviously not forgiven him for the slight. For once it is Bond who gets a well-deserved slap from a woman. Paris is a character that answers the question: whatever happened to all those women Bond ends up with at the close of his on-screen adventures? There is no specific character on which she is based, but her emotions speak for themselves. Despite Bond's quick departure from her life it is obvious that Paris still considers him her great love, when she realizes he is in danger, she risks her own life to warn him and to find out why Bond severed their relationship. Bond admits he left because she got too close They spend one night together before Paris is murdered on the orders of her husband.

At the same media party where Bond reacquaints himself with Paris, Bond meets Wai Lin (Michelle Yeoh), an agent of the Chinese People's External Security Force posing as a member of the New China News Agency. Wai Lin is every bit Bond's equal in the art of espionage, possibly superior in many areas. She can scuba-dive, fight, use an array of weapons, and she is at least as calm as Bond when facing a seemingly suicidal leap off a Hanoi skyscraper. In fact, it is her idea to make the jump. She moves with grace – despite her arguments with Bond – during a blazingly fast motorcycle chase in which she and Bond must share the driving duties while handcuffed to each other. This scene pays homage to Alfred Hitchcock's classic, *The Thirty-Nine Steps* (1935), where Robert Donat's Richard Hannay is handcuffed to a reluctant Pamela played by Madeleine Carroll.

If anything, Wai Lin occupies a position of greater importance in the story than Bond until the final battle where she is captured aboard Elliot Carver's stealth ship. Bond is constantly trying to partner with her. Only when Wai Lin extracts a guarantee from Bond that he is not on a personal mission of revenge for the death of Paris does she agree to co-operate.

The pair work as a team, and remarkably, have no sexual interplay, or even much flirting before the film draws to a close. Additionally, Wai Lin strikes a new path for a Bond woman. Her secret agent skills allow her to accomplish her goals without ever using her sex appeal as an obvious weapon (although Elliot Carver seems enchanted with her when they meet, Wai Lin does not act provocatively, in the way that Pam Bouvier does with Professor Joe Butcher in *Licence to Kill*, or the way Jinx distracts guards by partially disrobing in *Die Another Day*). Wai Lin's sex appeal comes from her abilities and her confidence and not just her physical beauty. She carries just as much self-assurance as 007, and she carries it well.

Michelle Yeoh (opposite and above with Pierce Brosnan): 'With the character of Wai Lin it firmly endorses Bond as a man of the Nineties who is strong, who is confident of who he is. We are both on a job, and whoever can do it, does it.'

The World Is Not Enough

In 1999, *The World Is Not Enough* portrayed a very different kind of conflict for James Bond involving a powerful emotional relationship with a remarkable woman, Elektra King (Sophie Marceau). As the film begins, Elektra's father, the oil magnate Sir Robert King, is killed in an explosion at MI6 headquarters and Bond is saddled with the knowledge that he is partially to blame – it was Bond who unwittingly brought the lethal bomb into the inner sanctum of British Intelligence. Bond subsequently learns that the murder of King was related to the kidnapping of Elektra by a terrorist named Renard some time earlier.

While researching the case Bond watches a post-escape video made of a traumatized Elektra. He is so moved by the image and his feelings of responsibility for her father's death, that he tries to touch the tear on her cheek shown on the computer monitor. M is concerned for Elektra's safety, given that Renard is still at large, and Bond wants the assignment to protect her.

Unfortunately, a shoulder injury prevents him from receiving the mission until he seduces MI6 medical officer, Dr Molly Warmflash (Serena Scott Thomas), who clears him for duty.

M gives Bond the mission, along with the caveat that he is not to sleep with Elektra under any circumstances. What neither of them realize is that Elektra does not need protection because she is actually in league with Renard. She seduced the terrorist while she was in captivity once she realized her father would not pay a ransom to free her. She then helped Renard plot and carry out her father's murder. Now she plans to use Renard again in a plot to give her sole control of all oil being piped west from the Caspian Sea. In short, she is the villain, the evil mastermind behind the story.

Elektra is an accomplished seductress, playing the strong, confident superwoman when it suits, and displaying a childlike fragility when that facade will help achieve her goals. The combination is exhilarating and enticing for 007. As producer Barbara Broccoli said to the writers Neal Purvis and Robert Wade during development of the script, 'Bond thinks he has found Tracy [whom he married in *On Her Majesty's Secret Service*], but he's really found Blofeld.'

Elektra toys with the concept of Bond's sexual and emotional invincibility. Here, for once, 007 cannot trust his judgement. His feelings for Elektra endanger the mission and his own survival. One of the largest obstacles he must overcome is his own attachment to the villain. It is a remarkable and decidedly different perspective on both Bond and the traditional expectations of the role of a woman in a Bond film.

Fortunately for 007 there is another, more traditional Bond Girl in the film, Dr Christmas Jones (Denise Richards), a physicist with the International Decommissioning Agency. At an underground test chamber, where she works, Dr Jones notices that Bond's credentials are forgeries. As a result she has guards subdue Bond and inadvertantly allows Renard to steal a nuclear device. She spends much of the rest of the film trying to make up for that unintentional error. Her expertise with nuclear weapons makes her a perfect ally, and her willingness to take on the tough physical aspects of the adventure earns Bond's respect and makes her a good match for 007.

Sophie Marceau: 'The role of Elektra is just like a
gift. it's an action film but is a very feminine part.'

Halle Berry as Jinx (opposite) and (above) with Miranda
Frost played by Rosamund Pike in *Die Another Day*.

'SHE WAS VERY INTELLIGENT. SHE WAS BOND'S EQUAL ... SHE HAD TO SAVE HIM A FEW TIMES IN THE MOVIE. BOND AND JINX HAD A GREAT PARTNERSHIP'

HALLE BERRY ON JINX

Die Another Day

The women in *Die Another Day* brought Bond into the twenty-first century. Miranda Frost (Rosamund Pike) and Jinx (Halle Berry) are both accomplished secret agents.

Former Olympic fencing champion Miranda Frost works for MI6 as a mole within the organization of multi-billionaire villain Gustav Graves. As her name implies, she is emotionally cold and remains unimpressed with Bond when the pair meet. Frost is a *femme fatale* who is, in fact, a double agent working for Graves. She sleeps with Bond in order to win his trust, then uses that trust to protect Graves and ultimately betray 007.

Bond meets the beautiful and mysterious Jinx as she strides out of the sea in Cuba (an *homage* to Honey Ryder's unforgettable entrance in *Dr. No*). She seduces Bond in the same way he has seduced others taking pleasure where she finds it. She sleeps with Bond on her own terms, leaving him before he's awake. As she says when they first meet, her relationships 'just don't seem to last'. Bond follows Jinx to an island clinic where he discovers she is a lethal spy. But Bond does not know on whose side she is fighting or if he can trust her after she abandons him during a gun battle on the island.

Indeed, the theme of trust and identity runs throughout the film. Even MI6 is not certain they can trust Bond after he is tortured and imprisoned by the North Koreans. The world, it turns out, cannot trust Graves and his Icarus satellite, which he purportedly built for purely humanitarian purposes. In contrast, it is the trust that develops between Bond and Jinx that becomes the emotional fulcrum of the last half of the story.

Jinx and Bond eventually realize they are both on a mission to expose Graves's nefarious plan, they both save each other's lives when their identities are exposed during the unveiling of Icarus at a party in Iceland. Jinx proves to be an adept partner. She has the same skills and confidence as Bond and is as comfortable flying the world's largest aircraft as she is at carrying out a cold-blooded assassination. At the film's climax, she and Bond both battle with equal verve for victory and survival. The filmmakers cut between Bond fighting Graves, and Jinx grappling with Miranda Frost, whom she kills. She is self-assured enough to use her sex appeal as a weapon, but not as a crutch. Jinx is a perfect counterpart for Bond in the new millenium, revealing just as much style, spark and talent as 007.

The other women

There are two other women in Bond's life who deserve special mention. The first is Miss Moneypenny, the secretary to M, Bond's chief. Moneypenny appears in Fleming's novels, but less often than the secretary to the double-O section, Loelia Ponsonby. Since the real Loelia Ponsonby was a friend of Fleming's (and also the Duchess of Westminster) who did not wish her fictional namesake to appear in a film, Fleming retired Ponsonby from his future novels at the time of the 1962 shooting of *Dr. No* in Jamaica. Mary Goodnight – the later heroine of the novel (and film) *The Man With The Golden Gun* – took over the job in *On Her Majesty's Secret Service*.

In the EON-produced Bond films three actresses have played Moneypenny – Lois Maxwell in the first fourteen films, Caroline Bliss during the Dalton era, and the appropriately named Samantha Bond in the Brosnan movies. Each actress has maintained a certain core element of the cinematic Moneypenny, but each incarnation of the character has also been different. Even in the first fourteen performances by Lois Maxwell, the character shows many changes in her relationship with James Bond.

In *Dr. No*, Moneypenny helps cement the notion of James Bond's sexual irresistibility. Bond meets Moneypenny when he arrives at headquarters for his meeting with M, a scene that comes in between the two scenes with Sylvia Trench. Moneypenny greets Bond, irritated that she has been unable to locate him in an emergency. Bond playfully flirts with her, but the dialogue makes it clear that this tête-à-tête signals the limit of their relationship.

Moneypenny is refreshingly sophisticated, not some demure, lovelorn office worker. Maxwell herself insisted the character avoid those cinematic clichés. She asked not to have to put her hair in a bun, or be forced to wear glasses or have a pencil over her ear. Although glasses did show up in *The Man With The Golden Gun*, her character seemed as if she were part of Bond's world and not an outsider looking in.

Despite these good intentions, Bond's reputation as the ultimate sex object for women quickly began to influence the way audiences viewed Moneypenny and the way she was written and played. In *Goldfinger* and *Diamonds Are Forever*, Moneypenny jokes about marriage and seems genuinely to wish Bond would sweep her off her feet. Bond appears openly irritated with her forwardness in *You Only Live Twice*, where she tries to get him to repeat the recognition code with the Japanese Secret Service – 'I love you' – while staring into her eyes. In films like *From Russia With Love*, *Thunderball* and *Live And Let Die*, her overtures appear as the teasing flirtations of a friend who enjoys more amusement than heartache from Bond's potentially licentious adventures. In fact, she helps conceal James Bond's night-time playmate in his closet in the later film.

Live And Let Die also marked a notable change in Moneypenny's relationship to 007. For the rest of the Roger Moore era, she exhibits none of the flirtatious behaviour of previous films, although she enjoys teasing Bond about his adventures, amorous and otherwise.

In *Octopussy*, Maxwell's penultimate performance as Moneypenny, Penelope Smallbone (Michaela Clavell) is half-heartedly introduced as an assistant. Smallbone had departed by the next film, and so did Lois Maxwell by 1987's *The Living Daylights*.

Caroline Bliss's Moneypenny returned to the earlier tradition of flirting with Bond. Unfortunately, the filmmakers forgot Lois Maxwell's dictum about playing Moneypenny against the clichés. Bliss, a spectacularly beautiful actress, performed as Moneypenny beneath a hair bun, glasses and with the ever-ready pencil behind her ear. She was efficient, but with an air of fragility beneath her props. Her character never quite recovered from offering to have Bond over to listen to her Barry Manilow music collection in *The Living Daylights*.

In 1995, Samantha Bond brought back the original feel of the Bond – Moneypenny relationship with a Nineties twist. The good-natured flirting is between friends, and Moneypenny's comment to Bond in *GoldenEye* that 'one day you have to make good on your innuendos', sounds more like bluff-calling than her wish for reality. Moneypenny takes great pleasure in teasing Bond about his girlfriends and the sexual adventures of his assignments. By *The World Is Not Enough*, she begins to make jokes about marriage, asking if James brought her an engagement ring from Spain. Samantha Bond's Moneypenny obviously harbours fantasies involving 007, as can be seen when she is discovered using Q's virtual reality training chamber in *Die Another Day*. Even in fantasy, the sight of Bond finally delivering a passionate kiss to Moneypenny seemed improper but felt well-deserved after forty years of anticipation.

M is Moneypenny's boss, and in the Brosnan films, the role is played by Dame Judi Dench. While the move to have a woman succeed Bernard Lee and Robert Brown was clearly inspired by Stella Rimington's tenure as Director General of MI5, the question of how to portray her was a far more interesting problem. Because of the sexual tension between Bond and so many of the women he encounters in the course of his cinematic adventures, the filmmakers faced a specific question – would a change in M's gender also mean a change in the nature of Bond's relationship with M? The answer was both yes and no.

Bringing in a female M only strengthened and clarified the dynamic Bond has had with his superior since *Dr. No*. The routine of M's measured reaction to Bond's exasperatingly roguish behaviour had become comic in the Seventies and Eighties, and it was hard to regain the wonderful tension from earlier Bonds in the more serious Timothy Dalton films. Bond was clearly better at doing his job than M was at telling him how to do it. This diminished M, and, ultimately, made Bond seem more like a loose cannon than Her Majesty's loyal servant.

Samantha Bond (with Pierce Brosnan from *Die Another Day*): 'I like to think that Moneypenny now meets James very much as an equal. She's equally witty. I like to think that she meets him sexually as an equal, too.'

'WITH ALL RESPECT, M, I DON'T THINK YOU HAVE THE BALLS FOR THIS.' 'PERHAPS THE ADVANTAGE IS I DON'T HAVE TO THINK WITH THEM ALL THE TIME'

ADMIRAL ROEBUCK AND M IN *TOMORROW NEVER DIES*

With a female M, the filmmakers found a way to reintroduce the delicate conflict between 007 and his superior. The conflict returns not by having Bond emasculated by a tough female boss, nor by having Bond patronizingly mock a strident female's attempts to keep him in line; it comes by having 007 confront a character every bit as strong and accomplished as himself. Bond's conflicts with her (and hers with him) are philosophical, not based on gender.

In *GoldenEye*, M is described by Bill Tanner as 'the evil queen of numbers'. But M, like all the great Bond women, is stronger than an initial description might suggest. She understands Bond, and as she tells him, she has 'no compunction about sending you to your death'. Conversely, she also values life, including Bond's. She admits to not liking his methods, and even not liking Bond himself, but she also understands that when the going gets tough, she wants Bond there to do the dirty work.

M does not solicit friendships in the 'Old Boy' network of British Intelligence. She commands respect through her exactingly high standards, unflinching willingness to make tough choices, and her record of accomplishment. She can confront admirals without flinching, and cannot be swayed by compliments. In *GoldenEye*, she cautions Bond that his reckless methods may not be the best solution to a problem. 'Don't make it personal', she states flatly. In *Tomorrow Never Dies*, she finds the balance, tempering Admiral Roebuck's bellicose instinct to launch a war by endorsing Bond's ability to stop one.

Like the M of Fleming's Bond – particularly the short story 'For Your Eyes Only' – she finds herself confronted with a very personal situation in *The World Is Not Enough*. Assassins manage to kill her friend Sir Robert King inside MI6 headquarters. M's hope for redemption for MI6's mistakes ultimately allows King's daughter, Elektra, to betray her. In captivity, M shows her resourcefulness, and Bond's respect for her is noted when, as he chases Elektra through the Maiden's Tower in Istanbul, he pauses to shoot the lock off M's cell before killing Elektra.

In *Die Another Day*, M's cold ability to detach is clear when she refuses to allow Bond back into MI6 after his captivity in North Korea. She is willing to send Bond for detainment on the Falklands, branded as a potentially damaged and thus dangerous enemy of the Crown. It is only through Bond's personal mission of vengeance that he is able to earn back M's respect, although he does not gain her full trust until he is able to expose one of her own agents, Miranda Frost, as a mole working for Gustav Graves.

Many observers over the years noted that Bond's relationship with M was like that of a young man's contentious relationship with his father. Bond respects M as would a son, but with a similar determination to find ways to assert individuality, to rebel and succeed on his own terms. If this is the case, why does the dynamic between a male Bond and a female M feel so appropriate?

Ian Fleming, James Bond's creator, lost his father as a young boy. He had no father to rebel against during adolescence and young adulthood. He did, though, have his mother, Eve, who by all accounts was a force of nature. She instilled fear, respect, and devotion in her sons, although Ian certainly rebelled against her authority on occasions. Could Fleming's relationship with his mother have influenced Bond's with his superior? One clue may reside in Fleming's letters to Eve. They were always addressed to 'M'.

Judi Dench (*Die Another Day*) on the relationship between Bond and M: 'In *GoldenEye*, M and Bond tolerated each other, perhaps, but I think it's got fonder over the years.'

2 THE ALLURE

There are films that become memorable through a series of happy accidents and then there are the James Bond movies. One does not enjoy phenomenal success for over four decades by happenstance. Each 007 adventure is given careful consideration before it is committed to film. Over the history of James Bond, no other part of Bond's world has received more attention than the allure of the Bond Girls.

Many facets combine to create the unique Bond Girl allure. The sexually charged humour, the risqué flirting as well as their confident self-awareness. Most of the Bond Girls have goals that set them apart from 007. I enjoy watching Bond and the women matching wits, trying to challenge each other. All those elements make the women stronger characters, and to me, more alluring.

When I was cast to star as Kara Milovy with Timothy Dalton, I felt it was important for my character to be feminine. I played a cellist, so they gave me a classical look. I didn't have a leather catsuit like Michelle Yeoh had as the adventurous Wai Lin or a slit dress with chaotic Byzantine patterns that reflected the inner anger of Elektra King as played by Sophie Marceau. I wore clothes with clean, elegant lines and sported a classical hairstyle. The outfits were quite prim, and Kara's look reflected her unjaundiced view of the world.

It took nearly the entire film for Bond and Kara to fall for each other. For characters whose story must move more quickly, the filmmakers design a look to communicate emotions, desire and allure.

In *Goldfinger*, it takes less than three minutes for James Bond to draw Jill Masterson into a kiss after he meets her. The filmmakers made actress Shirley Eaton instantly alluring. When Bond first sees Jill, she is lying on her stomach on a chaise, in black bra and pants — a shot designed to show off her well-toned backside. The next shot features Jill in close-up looking through binoculars. Now Jill has turned on her side just far enough so that her décolletage is perfectly framed. In two carefully constructed shots, the filmmakers have made certain that every man and woman watching the film understands the physical aspect of her allure. Jill's black underwear hints at a potentially villainous nature and her connection to the villain. When the film cuts to Bond's hotel suite, Jill now wears Bond's baby-blue pyjama top, and she looks as sweet as a farmer's daughter.

From the beautiful lingerie worn by Tiffany Case in *Diamonds Are Forever* to the cloaked hats and hoods worn by Grace Jones in *A View To A Kill*, the Bond Girls have always looked alluring in ways that reveal their characters. It is a carefully created image that shows a Bond Girl is more than just another pretty face.

Maryam d'Abo

Shirley Eaton: 'I hope the Bond films never lose the kind of titillation and sexiness of the glamorous woman. So many films and so many things today are so realistic that they lose the mystery. They lose, I think, the sensual aspect.'

'I HAVE TO SAY THAT I ACTUALLY LIKE THAT I HAVE ONE OF THE MORE OBSCENE NAMES'

LOIS CHILES ON HOLLY GOODHEAD IN *MOONRAKER*

The challenge

THE BOND GIRLS CONSTANTLY challenge the sexual status quo as well as challenging Bond himself. That challenge presents a key element of the allure of Bond Girls.

In *Goldfinger*, James Bond wakes up to the sight of a woman holding a gun on him. She introduces herself with the now famous line, 'My name is Pussy Galore.' Even forty years later, the moment still fills viewers with a sense of disbelief at its audacity. The power in the scene obviously comes partially from just the use of the word 'pussy' in a way that tacitly acknowledges its ignominious slang definition. To a greater degree, it also comes from the way the name is presented. In the novel, the reader first encounters the name on a meeting schedule handed to James Bond. In a lesser film, a male character would tell James Bond that Goldfinger is working with a woman named Pussy Galore – wink, wink, nudge, nudge. Fortunately, the filmmakers ignored both these paths, choosing instead to make the character's potential weakness – a laughably sexually charged name – her strength.

Miss Galore does not exhibit any naïveté about the name. Quite the contrary, she is proud of it. Even if one were to assume that this woman was actually given the name at birth, she certainly didn't retain it out of a sense of family pride. No, her name gives her power, particularly over men. It declares a steel-nerved confidence to one and all. The word 'pussy' ceases to be a vulgar term of objectification and becomes a weapon, just as lethal as the contrastingly phallic gun in her hand.

The name is a challenge to Bond and to viewers. It is as if the filmmakers dared the audience to be confident enough to play along, to say the name without embarrassment. Bond rises to the challenge, repeating the name often with near casual indifference. In reality many in the press could not overcome their natural embarrassment. As Honor Blackman remembered, 'I had great difficulty with some interviewers because they wouldn't say the name. I used to quite deliberately say, "Oh, you mean Pussy?" And they used to die.'

Other Bond women have embraced double entendre names with similar verve. In interviews, Lois Chiles, who played Holly Goodhead, usually takes on an air of mock innocence. When asked about her character's name, she has often responded, 'It could mean that I'm smart, right?' When pressed, Chiles admits, 'I have to be honest. I have to say that I actually like that I have one of the more obscene names.'

Lois Chiles (above, with Roger Moore) on playing Holly Goodhead in *Moonraker*: 'This was an intelligent Bond woman, so I thought this could be fun.'

Famke Janssen, who played Xenia Onatopp (opposite) on how she approached fighting James Bond in *GoldenEye*: 'I worked with the stunt guys on that for a while, and I just wanted to make sure that it looked like I could kick his ass if I wanted to.'

Chiles says she enjoyed playing a character who, in name, followed on from Pussy Galore. 'The names are such a Bond tradition and are humorous in a way. They carry the tongue-in-cheek quality of the films themselves.'

Serena Scott Thomas of *The World Is Not Enough* also loves the allure of the Bond Girl names. 'It's just so classic to play the doctor he seduces. And the name! Dr Molly Warmflash. Actually, to be quite honest with you, I couldn't resist.'

When Halle Berry told actor Samuel Jackson that she was going to star in a Bond film, he joked that her character should have a Fleming-esque name like Cinnamon Buns. Halle later told reporters that the name became something of a joke on the set.

Famke Janssen said of her character's name – Xenia Onatopp – 'It suits the Bond genre. She's on top of men, on top of everything. It's suitable; it's not subtle.'

Some actresses have shied away from risqué names. Michelle Yeoh came up with the name Wai Lin which she felt would be acceptable to Asian audiences. Maud Adams admits she took pause when confronted with her character's name. 'I did have some reservation about the name. I said, "My God! I mean, that name as a title!" But then, of course, when I realized that 'Octopussy' really was the title of one of [Ian Fleming's] short stories, I sort of accepted the name.'

The names, whether they are sexually charged or just have a ring of elegance, like Tiffany Case or Solitaire, are far from the only challenge these women present. The Bond Girls, in their own way, have stood apart from traditional roles of women in society. A 1964 press release for *Goldfinger* claims that 'what makes a James Bond girl' is her bad girl image. In *Goldfinger*, for instance, there isn't a one you'd take home to mother.'

Famke Janssen on Xenia: 'She is really somebody who broke out of her environment and tried to be one of the guys.'

'SHE MIGHT SLEEP WITH MEN, OBVIOUSLY DID, BUT IT WOULD BE ON HER TERMS AND NOT THEIRS'

BOND ON DOMINO IN *THUNDERBALL*

Honor Blackman immediately understood that her character's allure was her lack of subservience. 'When you look at Pussy Galore she had an airforce of her own. She flew a plane ... She was Girl Power.'

Women used to think, as Bond producer Barbara Broccoli puts it, that 'traditionally a man sees a woman and says, "She's pretty, I'll go talk to her."' Today she thinks, 'women have now realized what men have known all along. Confidence and feeling comfortable with yourself are actually very attractive.'

From this confidence Bond women evolved who could and would do virtually anything. Richard Rayner, writing in *Esquire* in 1995, humorously mixed and matched elements from various characters, but he got the tone right when he stated:

> Good Bond Girls tend to be PhDs in particle physics or reluctant Soviet spies posing as concert cellists ... whereas bad Bond Girls dress in leather, do kung fu (sometimes good ones do this, too), slap around NATO jet pilots and then fill them full of junk from a hypodermic, and snuff out their enemies or no-longer-useful allies with rockets fired from between their legs as they ride giddily on powerful motorcycles.

Even though the Bond Girls can play just as rough as the boys in action films, do not mistake them for the overtly gender-neutral female characters in many films of the Nineties and beyond. No, the Bond Girls do not easily relinquish their feminine side. Thus, their challenge is decidedly sexual. They understand the power of sex, which is in itself appealing to men and women, just as Bond's sexual attractiveness is part of his allure.

The most memorable Bond Girls throw down the gauntlet when it comes to sex. Bond must earn his pleasure. He must rise to the challenge they present. This notion appeared directly in Fleming's novels:

'He felt the sexual challenge all beautiful lesbians have for men' – Bond's reaction to Pussy Galore in *Goldfinger*.

'She might sleep with men, obviously did, but it would be on her terms and not theirs' – Bond on Domino in *Thunderball*.

'She was beautiful in a devil-may-care way, as if she kept her looks for herself and didn't mind what men thought of them ... [her looks] seemed to say, "Sure, come on and try, but brother, you better be the tops"' – Bond on Tiffany Case in *Diamonds Are Forever*.

This sexual challenge goes right back to gender roles. Fleming's former agent, Peter Janson-Smith, described a Bond Girl as 'a woman who behaves like a man, but is still very much a woman'.

Claudine Auger (Domino in *Thunderball*) was born with the unlikely name of Claudine Oger. She won the title of Miss France in 1958, competing in the Miss World competition where she was first runner-up.

'BOND IS A KIND OF FANTASY IN A REAL WORLD WHICH IS A FANTASTIC OPPORTUNITY FOR AN ACTOR ... YOU CAN REALLY GO FOR IT AND OVERACT AS MUCH AS YOU LIKE'

SOPHIE MARCEAU

That is the yin and yang, the wonderful dichotomy of these characters. They are unique because they are what we want and yet not what we expect. In the more sexually repressed early Sixties, Sylvia Trench tries to pick up Bond in the casino just like a man. Honey Ryder's masculine confidence mixes beautifully with her feminine manner. As Bond says admiringly to Domino in *Thunderball*, 'Most girls just paddle around. You swim like a man.'

The Bond Girls say to women, 'Embrace your sexuality, experiment, explore, break free of the bounds of society.' To men, the Bond women say, 'Do not fear that a strong, confident, sexually assured woman will make you weaker. No, she will be the best thing ever to happen to you.'

Of course, crossing traditional gender boundaries does cause confusion for some traditionalists. For example, the character of Pussy Galore was so strong and so unique that, combined with Honor Blackman's Cathy Gale persona popularized in *The Avengers*, an absurd rumour started in England. That rumour became so widespread that it led to Blackman's strangest interview.

'We got to the studio literally five minutes before I was due on,' Blackman recalled. 'We were on directly after the news ... As the countdown started, the interviewer said, "What would you like me to ask you?" And I said, "I don't give a damn what you ask me. I like not to know." They started the countdown and he said, "Christ ... shit ... fuck," he was swearing on every figure of the countdown. I thought, "My God, this doesn't auger well." He was obviously shockingly nervous. So, the camera was on my finger [Blackman was wearing a jewelled finger ornament], and it pulled back, and he spoke too soon. I can't remember what the first question was that he asked me, but whatever it was, I answered him. And then he suddenly said, "Miss Blackman, what is it like being half male and half female?" At which I absolutely broke up. I had on a very low-cut dress, so I leaned forward and I said, "Which half did you have in mind for which?"'

If the Bond Girls are so unapproachable, so challenging, so willing to use their sexuality as a weapon, where are the pliant women, the eye candy that the Bond Girls are so often accused of being? They are the decorative Bond beauties, present in virtually all the early Bond films, but rarely in the leading roles. They may be patients at Blofeld's clinic in *On Her Majesty's Secret Service* or circus performers in *Octopussy*, or bathing girls in *You Only Live Twice*. These women make up another factor in the allure of the Bond Girls. They set the seductive mood of the films, paint the backdrop of sexual glamour and libidinous desire.

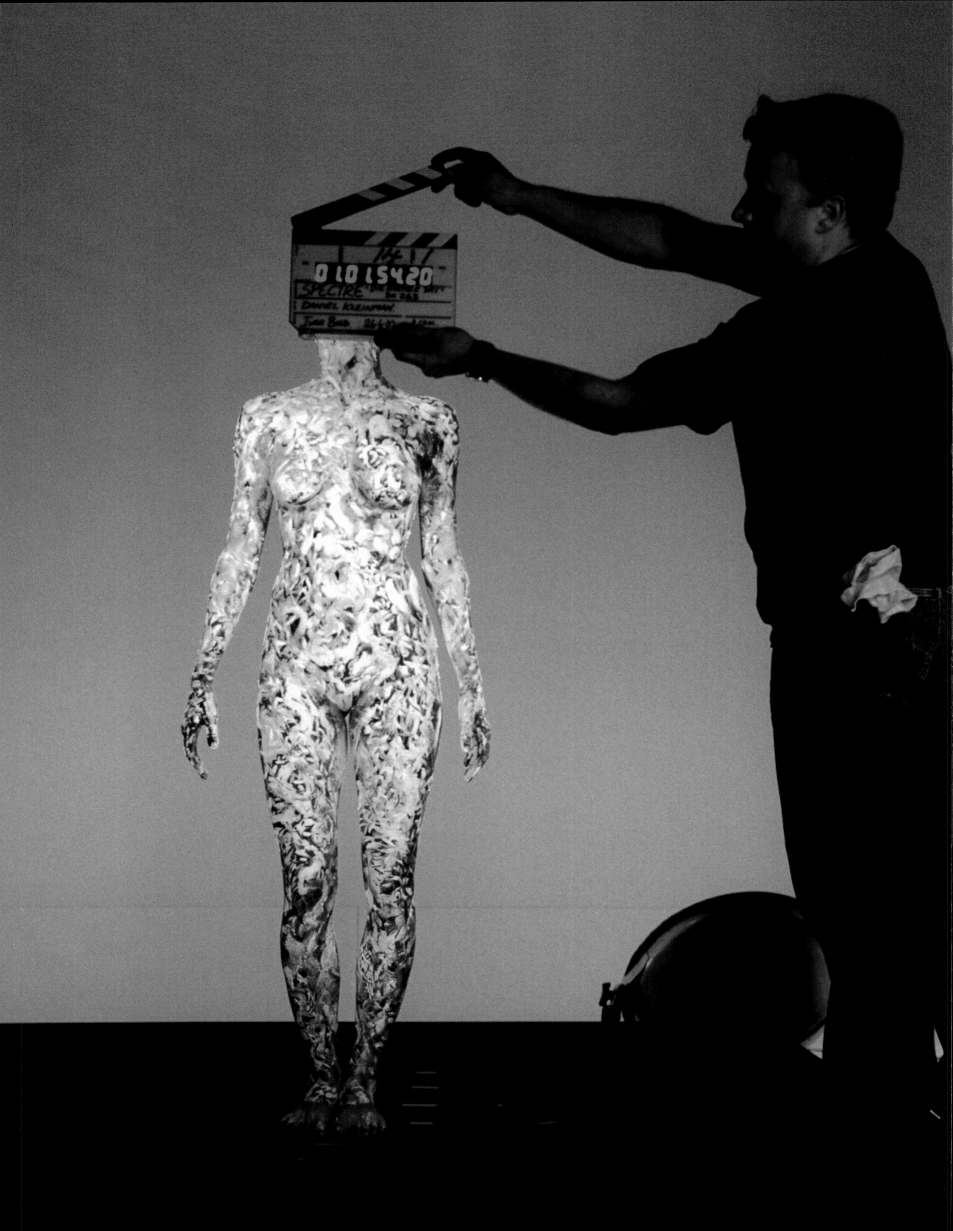

Pussy Galore's flying circus (above) prepares to take to the air.

The alluring female figures of the James Bond title sequences help set the scene of heightened sexuality in the films. A model stands ready (opposite) to perform for Daniel Kleinman's cameras for the innovative sequence in *Die Another Day*.

The female beauties populating Bond's world became a tradition starting with *Dr. No*, when Terence Young decided to cast tremendously attractive women in minor roles. Note the beautiful clerks at the Ministry of Intelligence communications room and particularly the raven-haired beauty who delivers the message to the foreman of signals. Young cast the 1961 Miss Jamaica, Marguerite LeWars, in a small but vital role. He also introduced the idea of having a lovely hotel clerk who looks longingly after 007 when he walks away from the front desk (played in *Dr. No* by Malou Pantera).

When Guy Hamilton came to direct *Goldfinger*, he started another tradition of beautiful women surrounding a pool or adorning a beach, often looking admiringly at 007. When filming the initial scenes for *Goldfinger* in Miami, Hamilton brought in local models to sun themselves in the background of the establishing and back-projection plate shots. In *Thunderball*, the women frolic behind Bond and Domino as he tries to entice her to sample some of his conch chowder. In *The Spy Who Loved Me*, bikini-clad women gather to watch Bond's Lotus sports car emerge from the deep. The importance of these glamorous extras grew to the point that the films of the Eighties often contained a separate credit listing for them. In *A View To A Kill*, just after the credits for 'The Snow Team', there is a listing for 'The Girls' – naming the many beautiful women who did

not get a speaking part. While bikinis around the pool may have been overplayed in the Eighties, scenes with a plethora of glamorous women have never disappeared. *The World Is Not Enough* achieved much the same effect of the poolside scenes by having Bond wear Q's version of X-ray specs in a casino, allowing him to see beneath the slinky dresses of the female patrons.

Another element of Bond's highly sexed world comes from the provocative title sequences by Maurice Binder (*Dr. No*, *Thunderball* to *Licence To Kill*), Robert Brownjohn (*From Russia With Love* and *Goldfinger*) and Daniel Kleinman (*GoldenEye* to *Die Another Day*) which have never lost their allure. They manage to excite both men and women with their dreamy and often fetishistic imagery. In many countries, the titles were the most common target of the censor's scissors. Peter Hunt complained that because of the clear outline of one silhouetted woman's nipple, his director credit was missing in South Africa from *On Her Majesty's Secret Service*. Hunt was lucky. In Spain, *Thunderball* initially played with no titles. Binder, who was an amazing visual artist, was unrepentant. Asked in 1981 why he used silhouettes of naked women, he replied, 'Censorship. I can get away with a nude in silhouette and I can't get away with a nude for real.' In short, he was going to push the limits as far as he could.

Mise-en-scéne

Leave it to the French to come up with a way of separating the characters, dialogue, plot, music, editing, and acting from a film. They call everything that is left the *mise-en-scéne*. It is the world in which the story takes place and the way that world is presented to an audience. The 'Bond Girl world' may look like our world, but it is not. It is something more, a seductive setting where the sun shines a little brighter, the heart beats a little quicker, and all the things that hold us to our daily routines and mundane comforts become of little consequence.

Camille Paglia, the famous anti-feminist feminist as she likes to be called, remembers the first time she saw *Dr. No* in 1963. She immediately sensed the power of the film's *mise-en-scéne*. 'It was incredible. You felt you were in another world. The whole movie just wrapped you up and took you into this other world.'

Many films feature exotic locations, but the Bond films present them in a particularly seductive way. One of the reasons is that Bond is invariably entering the woman's world. For example, the lush Caribbean beach and waterfalls shown surrounding Honey Ryder in *Dr. No* 'belong' to her. Bond is the interloper, the tourist who gracefully brings the viewers into it. Similarly, Istanbul in *From Russia With Love* is Tatiana's territory. Bond meets Jill Masterson on her balcony in Goldfinger's hotel suite. In *The World Is Not Enough*, he first sees Elektra King at her father's funeral, then later at the site of her pipeline. Even in *Die Another Day*, writers Neal Purvis and Robert Wade conceived of Jinx by posing the question, 'What if James Bond walked into another character's movie?' Thus, Jinx knows much more about what is going on in Cuba and the secret DNA clinic on Los Organos than Bond.

The Ice Palace offered a setting that was not only visually spectacular, it also reflected the emotional coldness of Miranda Frost (Rosamund Pike, with Pierce Brosnan), a woman who willingly sleeps with James Bond in order to more effectively betray him later.

'I WAS SUPPOSED TO BE THE
GOOD ONE, AND GRACE JONES
WAS SUPPOSED TO BE THE EVIL
ONE, AND SO THEY DECIDED TO PUT
ME IN THESE RATHER CONSERVATIVE
THINGS ... I WOULD'VE LIKED TO HAVE
WORN A CATSUIT OR SOMETHING'

TANYA ROBERTS

Why is this important? All of these locations are presented in a clean, opulent way. These women don't live in a little bedsit a couple of streets from the factory. Their world is one we want to live in. Everyone wants to spend a night in Octopussy's bed. Everyone wants to make weightless love in space. We all see the world of the Bond Girl as more immediate and exhilarating than our own. When Honey walks from the sea, or when she and Bond bathe in the waterfall, we want to live that moment, to seize it and hold it.

Honey Ryder's world is not some Hollywood studio creation. It is 'real', but only up to a point. One can visit Laughing Waters, the actual beach in Jamaica where Ursula Andress strode from the waves, but one can't live in Bond's reality. Bond's world is filled with magical elements, like a mechanical dragon, or a supertanker that eats submarines, or an island on a lake in India populated with a harem of fair maidens, or a palace made of ice. The magic and beauty of these worlds accentuates the magic and beauty of the women who live amidst such splendour.

Strip away the *mise-en-scéne* from *Dr. No*. All it takes is a quick look behind the Eden-like sense of luxury that surrounds Honey Ryder to make her character far less appealing. One would not even have to change a single line of dialogue. Place her on a prop-less stage. Have her tell the story of her life, of the loss of her father, her betrayal and rape by a family friend, her subsequent revenge upon her attacker,

and her isolation and alienation from the world. This is not a life any woman would choose to live, nor a description any man would find enticing. In *Dr. No*, the filmmakers create a world where Honey is seductive in addition to being impossibly attractive (she had a broken nose in Fleming's novel). This world is so idyllic that she can literally get away with murder.

When Tanya Roberts (Stacey Sutton in *A View To A Kill*) explains why the Bond Girls are considered among the sexiest women in the world, she immediately credits the *mise-en-scéne*. 'That's how the filmmakers make the Bond women appear. They are no different than any other, objectively. The point is that we're put in very sireny, sexy situations, and there's always a lot of money and a lot of fancy locations and fancy cars. So that's how we're perceived.'

Even those Bond women who are described as 'ordinary' are, in fact, placed in extraordinary worlds. Take Natalya Simonova in *GoldenEye*. Izabella Scorupco says Natalya was 'the most real character in this movie. I was trying not to think of my character as a Bond Girl ... I think that was the most important thing for me, to make her as human as possible.' Nonetheless, she works in a spectacular top-secret satellite control centre, entrusted with programming space hardware worth hundreds of millions of dollars. Her life is filled with secrets and amazing technology. Her *mise-en-scéne* of post-Cold War Russia, with all its chaos, is exotic and dangerous.

The myth

Because Bond exists in a cinematic world where all the hormones seem to be working overtime, his desire for one woman over another is an important reason audiences find the Bond women so interesting. Bond is the mythic irresistible alpha-male in the films. Those women who do resist his initial advances compel Bond to rise to their standards. Those women themselves become icons of irresistibility to the audience. They are the élite, the alpha-women. They are the Bond Girls we often best remember.

This brings us to the most important part of the allure of the Bond Girls, the reason they have survived throughout all social changes for women over the past forty-plus years. The Bond Girls are at once new, but in another way, they have been around as long as stories have been told. They are just the latest incarnations of the women who have forever appeared in tales of heroes, adventure, and sex. As Maud Adams says, the Bond stories are 'really a modern-day fairytale'.

The Bond women exist in the twilight between the real world and mythology. In 1964, Sean Connery spoke about their allure. 'There isn't a girl-next-door in the entire lot. And I suppose that's what appeals most to the men in the audience about Bond's playmates. They are so utterly unreal, the kind of women you meet only in your fantasies and your dreams.'

For millions of film-goers, the Bond stories represent the fantasies of our times. Bond lasts because the adventures are constructed like myths, and the Bond women are an essential ingredient of this mythology.

Luciana Paluzzi (Fiona Volpe in *Thunderball*) on what makes the Bond women memorable: 'All of them seem to be smart. They are not just an adornment. They always have a brain.'

Fleming made many references to the story of the patron saint of England, St George, in his novels. In *Moonraker*, Bond battles Sir Hugo Drax, whose German birth name is Hugo von der Drache. 'Drache' means 'dragon' in German. In *Dr. No*, Bond, with Honeychile Rider at his side, faces down a mechanical dragon in the marsh (the location of the dragon in the St George myth). In *Goldfinger*, as the villain displays a carton containing an atomic warhead, Bond urges himself into action:

> *This time it really was St George and the dragon. And St George had better get a move on and do something before the dragon hatched the little dragon's egg he was now nesting so confidently.*

In *The Spy Who Loved Me*, it is not Bond who sees the parallel, but his lover, Vivienne Michel.

> *I think I know why I gave myself so completely to this man, how I was capable of it with someone I had met only six hours before. Apart from the excitement of his looks, his authority, his maleness, he had come from nowhere, like the prince in the fairy tales, and he had saved me from the dragon. But for him, I would now be dead, after suffering God knows what before ... But he had fought for my life as if it had been his own. And then, when the dragon was dead, he had taken me as his reward.*

In *On Her Majesty's Secret Service*, Tracy, Bond's bride, is a countess, whose name is Draco, another foreign derivation of dragon. Naturally, in the St George myth the damsel in distress is wearing her bridal gown as she awaits death from the dragon. She also is not just any beautiful woman. No, she is the princess, the most revered and powerful woman of the realm. In their own way, so are the Bond Girls.

Maud Adams (on location for *Octopussy*): 'I think there is a lot in James Bond movies for women. I think that the women like to identify with the heroines because although they are very beautiful women, they are also women who are most often in charge of their own life. They usually give James Bond a helluva ride for his money.'

Camille Paglia sees another mythic parallel. 'James Bond is like Odysseus in Homer's poem who goes from place to place meeting villains, or being seduced by half-divine women.' Paglia agrees this mythic parallel is a key element in the attraction of Bond and the Bond Girls:

> There's a big difference in Bond's style of seduction compared to that of the kind of lounge lizard who draws women back to his bachelor pad in so many of those movies of the late Fifties and Sixties. With James Bond you feel that though he is enjoying the sexuality of the women, he's also honouring them. It's almost like Jupiter visiting the human realm in all of those many legends of the King Of The Gods enjoying human women!

Using Paglia's first analogy, one can see the *femme fatales* of the Bond films in the Sirens. In Bond's world, it is the *femme fatales*' sexual allure that is their song, and Bond, like Odysseus, has the chance to indulge without falling prey to the fate of those who have come before.

The Bond Girls resonate with us because they lead us back to epic stories. They inhabit Bond's world, a world much like our own but the colours are brighter and the stakes higher. They are part of the mythology of our modern world which helps us define our desires and modern fantasies. The Bond women's allure remains timeless because they are part of a tradition of stories that have been told since the beginning of time.

Eunice Gayson as Sylvia Trench (with Sean Connery in *Dr. No*) was the first Bond woman of the big screen. Dana Broccoli felt characters like Trench represented something new in films: 'The Bond women were nothing like the women in earlier films. It was the beginning of the sexual revolution and I think that the female audiences were welcoming the change as were the men.'

3 THE STARS

This is my story. It begins in the Twenties with a Georgian General fighting for the independence of his country against troops under the command of Lenin. The Soviets crushed the nascent battle for independence in Georgia. The General was forced to escape the Soviet regime and its infamous secret police, the KGB, fleeing to Paris at the invitation of the French Government.

The General was my grandfather. In 1987, I starred in *The Living Daylights*, a film that centred around a plot to make the British believe the KGB had reactivated Smersh and was murdering British agents. In the film, my character had the chance to lead soldiers into battle and help them defeat Soviet troops. My grandfather would have appreciated the irony!

My father was English. He fell ill when I was five so my mother had to work. She joined UNICEF, the United Nations Children's Fund for which Roger Moore has recently done so much great work. We lived in Paris, and later when UNICEF's headquarters moved, in Geneva. My mother was head of the greeting card division in Europe, which is one of the main ways UNICEF raises money. She travelled the world to investigate the plight of underprivileged children. I had the chance to meet extraordinary people through my mother's work. I can remember attending the Paris premiere of the musical *Hair*, giving flowers to Grace Kelly, Princess of Monaco. Another time, I sat on Peter Ustinov's lap during the taping of a programme about children of the world.

My mother wanted me to learn languages, experience different cultures and I travelled alone to visit her friends in Washington DC, San Francisco and New York. I was very fortunate in that I was able to see so much of the world at such a young age.

In my early teens, I realized I loved movies, storytelling, and the world of acting. After a short stint of studying photography in London, I enrolled in drama school. To pay for my studies I started work as a model in London, and soon I was working in television and theatre between England and France – I was lucky to be bilingual.

In 1986, I was asked by Barbara Broccoli if I would help screen-test a new actor as James Bond. We performed the famous bedroom scene from *From Russia With Love*. He did not get the part, but five months later I saw Barbara again. I had cut my hair for another film, and she barely recognized me. I looked very Slavic. She asked me to meet Cubby Broccoli, and soon after, they offered me the role of Kara in *The Living Daylights*.

Making the film was an amazing experience. I had the chance to travel to Vienna and Morocco. We were working from dawn until dusk in the desert at the Atlas Film Studios in Ouarzazate.

The scenery was breathtaking.

I could not resist the temptation of riding my white horse in this stunning landscape and therefore took off on my own during a lunch break, doing a Lawrence of Arabia! I got a stern lecture as the insurance did not allow me to ride off set.

However, I did a few of my own stunts. The roughest stunt was skidding down the snow in a converted cello case. There were handles built into the case for me to steer but it kept spinning out of control because Tim was heavier than me, I was certain I would guide us into a ravine. To make matters worse, the effects team had rigged small explosions to simulate bullets hitting all around.

I have an aversion to explosions. They send a wave of panic through me. These are things you learn about yourself when you work on a Bond film.

Probably the most important experience for me was the working relationship I had with Timothy Dalton. On some days the huge mechanics necessary to make a Bond film were overwhelming. Tim always took time to guide me through the scenes. He was great to work with, and he brought so much to the role of James Bond.

There are so many memories that go beyond what appears in the film. The work experiences, the new friendships, the exotic locations and especially the Moroccan sunsets.

As I said, this is my story. It is just one in the long line of adventures that so many actresses have had through the James Bond films.

Maryam d'Abo

Maryam d'Abo with Timothy Dalton sharing a laugh on location in Ouarzazate, Morocco.

Maryam d'Abo (above with Timothy Dalton): 'It took three days to film our escape in the cello case. It was the scariest scene for me because I felt out of control and I was the one steering and controlling the speed!'

Maryam d'Abo (opposite with Timothy Dalton): 'This was a great outfit to wear. I thought costume designer Emma Porteus was a wonderful person to work with. She brought simplicity and elegance to my character through the outfits she designed for Kara.'

THE ACTRESSES WHO HAVE appeared in the Bond films will tell you that they are very different from the Bond women characters they helped create. They do not believe that they are one of the glamorous, sophisticated, adventurous women of James Bond's world. Rather, they are mere mortals who wake up tired, get colds, run errands, and endure all the indignities our mundane world has to offer. Or so they would have us believe.

The lives of the Bond Girls are, naturally, larger than life. One expects dialogue like, 'I was schooled in France and Geneva' (this book's co-author, Maryam d'Abo) or back stories that include a brief marriage to the racing car-designing son of a Danish nobleman and a dashing heiress (Jill St John). Even the Bond women who appear to be of ordinary origins find themselves falling in love on transatlantic cruises (Lois Chiles) or while being carried down the slopes of the Italian Alps on the back of a champion skier (Lynn-Holly Johnson). You will find among them the daughter of a celebrated star of the Peking Opera (Tsai Chin) and the offspring of a famed novelist (Michaela Clavell).

These women have moved in worlds most of us only dream about. They have taken what cards they were dealt in life and played them well. If there is a reason they have been cast as remarkable women, it is because they are remarkable themselves.

Take, for example, two of the most famous women from the Bond film series – Ursula Andress and Lois Maxwell. Andress was unknown to film audiences, never having done much more than walk on a film set as a glorified extra. Maxwell, in contrast, had been acting for fifteen years with only modest success. Many writers have credited Andress's status as an icon solely to her beauty and Maxwell's success solely to the longevity of the series. In fact, both actresses were perfectly cast, and both were able to bring their own life-experience to their on-screen persona.

'I REALIZED I LOVED MOVIES. I LOVED STORYTELLING, AND I LOVED THE WORLD OF ACTING'

MARYAM D'ABO

Ursula Andress grew up in Switzerland, but at the age of fifteen she ran away with French actor Daniel Gelin. Andress and the recently divorced Gelin holed up in the most exclusive hotel in Rome while Andress's parents panicked. 'Brigitte Bardot and Roger Vadim hid me up in their hotel room, and Interpol went through the whole hotel trying to find me, because they knew very well I was there.'

'At the moment I was in that hotel, there was Marlon [Brando], there was Henri Vidal ... all the big actors were in that hotel. And we were a big, very, very, very mad crowd.

'You walk around in Rome, on the street and suddenly everybody says to you, "Oh, you have to be in the movies. Oh, you have to go to Cinecitta." You know, I couldn't believe it. I was laughing at it. I thought, it's just an Italian way to approach you.' Andress did two very small parts in Italian films, but it was the head of Paramount in Rome who flew her to England for four days of English lessons, acting lessons and a formal screen test. She did the test, signed a seven-year contract with Paramount, and was soon off to Hollywood. She was only seventeen, and she was petrified of acting.

On the Paramount Studios lot, Andress met the famed actor and photographer John Derek, and the pair soon married. 'I got a lot of offers, but then I was scared because they gave me roles in which I was supposed to show my feelings, my soul, my intimacy, and I got scared and I said no.' Eventually her contract was cancelled. Columbia then offered her a contract, which she accepted, but again she refused all parts offered. Columbia demanded she buy her contract back for $20,000, which Andress paid. She travelled the world with Derek. One day on a beach in Greece she posed for a photo that inspired Cubby Broccoli and Harry Saltzman to offer her the part of Honey Ryder in *Dr. No* without even so much as a face-to-face meeting or a screen test.

The script for *Dr. No* arrived in Los Angeles, but Andress refused to read it. 'One day Kirk Douglas came over, and we were all sitting around,' Andress remembers. 'He began to read, and we were all on the floor laughing and having fun with it, and then Kirk said, "Ursula, you have to do it." Thus, after six years of avoiding acting, Ursula finally accepted a role in a movie.

Andress might have been nervous about acting, but she was not nervous about who she was. The confidence and unselfconscious sense of beauty that radiated from her in *Dr. No* came from her own inner sense of self. Like Honey, Andress had struck out on her own. She had moved half way around the world, defied studio bosses and befriended some of the biggest names in Hollywood. As she herself said, 'I needed my freedom above everything since I was a child. I used to run away from home every day and I don't know why. It's in me. Freedom – it's like a magnet that draws me.'

When she strode on to that beach in Jamaica, Ursula Andress exuded a sense of freedom. The way she shook her hair, the way she moved, the way she breathed signalled this was someone who was unbound by the rules of society. She became in that moment what she valued most, an icon of personal freedom.

'The public saw me as perfect for the role. I didn't see myself as perfect for the role, but the public saw me as perfect.' Ursula Andress, 2002.

'WELL, WE'VE TESTED ANOTHER ACTRESS, AND QUITE FRANKLY, SHE LOOKS AS THOUGH SHE SMELLS OF SEX AND YOU LOOK AS THOUGH YOU SMELL OF SOAP'

TERENCE YOUNG ON LOIS MAXWELL

As M's secretary, Miss Moneypenny, Lois Maxwell maintained the longest tenure of any Bond Girl – fourteen films over twenty-three years. Her longevity in the part reflected her resilience in real life. As one would imagine of Moneypenny, Lois possesses a playful but circumspect air about herself. She has a spirit of determination and adventure that has served her well in real life as well as in her performances.

In Toronto as a young girl, Lois was cast in a children's radio programme without her parents' knowledge. 'When I was sixteen, I was recruited by the Canadian Army to join the Army Show as the gag girl for Wayne and Shuster, the famous Canadian comedians.' The show toured Canada and then went off to England for a number of months as the Second World War raged.

'My unit was being sent to Italy, and somehow headquarters found out that I was not yet eighteen … I went to London to the Royal Academy of Dramatic Art, and there I told Sir Kenneth Barnes that I didn't want to go back to Canada.' Maxwell had to go AWOL to attend the audition. She won the Lady Mountbatten scholarship to RADA but was arrested by the military police. It was only at the intervention of the Academy that she was allowed to stay in England.

Lois studied with Roger Moore at RADA. Her movie career took off almost immediately. She went to France to screentest for the part of the villainess in *Corridor of Mirrors*, a film directed by Terence Young.

'They had dressed me in a very slinky satin dress that was absolutely skin-tight with bosoms exposed and everything else.' Young later told her, '"You're not going to have the part." And I said, "Oh, Terence, why not?" And he said, "Well, we've tested another actress, and quite frankly, she looks as though she smells of sex and you look as though you smell of soap."'

Maxwell worked consistently, although she never broke through as a major star. When her husband suffered a massive heart attack at the age of forty, Maxwell knew she needed to make money for the family. 'I really needed a part as fast as they could find one for me, because we were pretty broke,' Maxwell recalled. Terence Young offered her the choice of two parts in *Dr. No*, both of which he felt would be recurring characters in the Bond films – Sylvia Trench or Miss Moneypenny. Lois naturally chose the character who smelled of soap.

Maxwell's performance as Moneypenny was successful because it reflected her own ability to handle crisis with aplomb. She played Moneypenny as a woman who understood Bond's dalliances on his missions. Part of her wanted to play the seductress, but inside she was more comfortable baking an 'angel cake' (as Miss Moneypenny offers to do for Bond in *Goldfinger*).

Lois Maxwell and Ursula Andress were both remarkable women before they hit the age of twenty, but they were not alone.

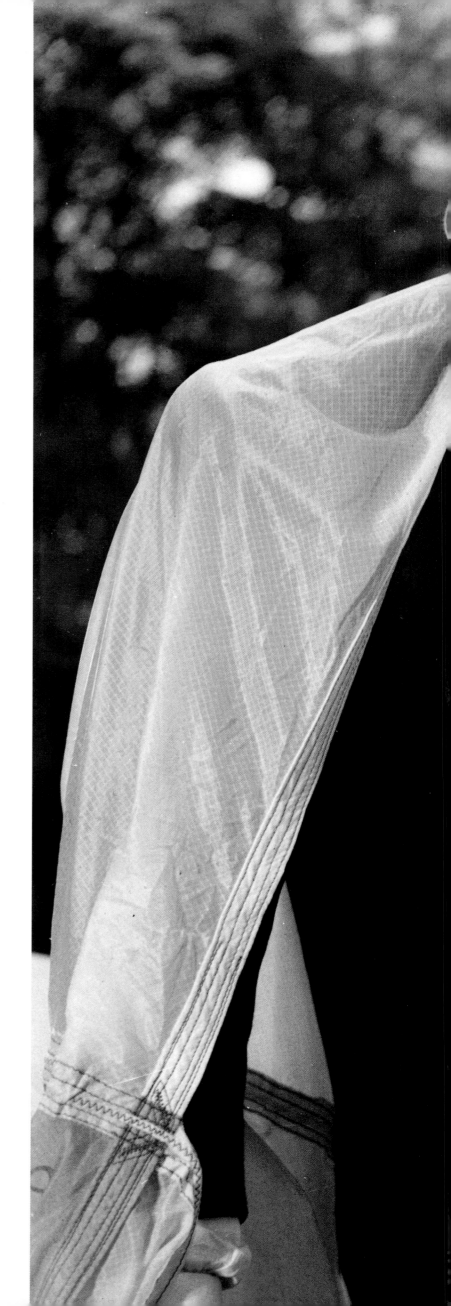

Despite a string of good girl 'English Rose' roles early in her career, Honor Blackman possessed the same sense of masculine self-reliance as her character, Pussy Galore in *Goldfinger*. 'I did knock out two boys because they bullied my brother,' she said. 'My right upper cut was absolutely terrific.' As the leather-clad adventuress Cathy Gale in *The Avengers*, Blackman not only became the most popular woman on British television, she also learned judo, which she performed on the cement floor of the studio. Blackman ended up with bruises each week, but some of the stuntmen she fought were in a worse state. For one episode Blackman was to run up a hill and kick her pursuer in the face. Technical mistakes required that the scene be performed over and over. On the fifth take, Blackman let out the kick too quickly. 'His eyes went completely crossed. I split his nose open and you could see he was gone, totally gone. He still remembered to run around and fight me for the shovel and fall back, but then he was out for seven and a half minutes.'

When asked, 'So you were Pussy Galore's character in real life?' Blackman replies, 'Yes. Yes, I was.' Blackman was also a very experienced actress, having appeared in over twenty films, including the blockbusters *A Night to Remember* and *Jason and the Argonauts*.

Jill St John's portrayal of the pragmatic Tiffany Case in *Diamonds Are Forever* reflects her own sense of pragmatism. 'I was born in Los Angeles ... and I've been acting since I was four years old,' Jill says. 'I certainly don't find it any nastier than any other big business. I think all big business is the same. It's bottom line.'

Like Tiffany Case, Jill is smart, completing two years of college by the time she was eighteen. She also enjoys the good life – and has an attraction (though not always romantic) to men who possess the suave and debonair demeanour of James Bond. She was once married to multi-millionaire Lance Reventlow and linked to Henry Kissinger at the height of his power. Her current husband, Robert Wagner, was once considered by Cubby Broccoli for the role of Bond.

Sean Connery and Honor Blackman in the final sequence of *Goldfinger*.

Lois Chiles (opposite and above, with Roger Moore in *Moonraker*) on the beauty of the Bond women: 'It's very diverse. we have an image of being very glamorous and mysterious, and I think really that comes from the Bond franchise itself. We are perceived that way because we are Bond Girls.'

Lois Chiles (Holly Goodhead in *Moonraker*) grew up in the small town of Alice, Texas, but her background was far from provincial. After falling in love on a transatlantic ocean crossing at the age of eighteen, Chiles was nearly married at twenty. 'I had this raging energy and I didn't know really what it was. What it ended up being was the need to be an artist.'

Chiles decided, however, to finish school in New York City, but her combination of beauty and her need for artistic outlet quickly changed her plans. 'I was in the snack bar at school on the first day, and *Glamour* magazine came around. They were looking for people for their college issue, and they chose me.'

After two years of top assignments, a boyfriend urged Chiles to take acting classes. The results were improbable to say the least. 'I ended up with a little boy that nobody wanted to be his partner. He said, "We can rehearse at my friend Billy Barnes's house." I called over there and Billy Barnes said, "I like your name. Would you like to come to my cocktail party tomorrow night?" and I said sure. And I went to his cocktail party. I opened the door and it was everybody that was in New York theatre or film at that moment. So three months after that Billy Barnes became an agent at the biggest agency, and he called me and said, "Would you like to be my first client?"'

Within four years, Chiles had landed a significant role in *The Way We Were* followed by *The Great Gatsby*. She was, like her character, always ending up in the most remarkable places, acting as though it was the most natural thing in the world for her to be there. Without a script, Chiles herself would not proclaim to be a NASA scientist (she makes no bones about her lack of interest in technology and often refers to the Moonraker space shuttle as 'the plane' in interviews). Nonetheless, Chiles does have a devil-may-care attitude about her that is a key attraction to the character of Holly Goodhead.

'I HAD THIS RAGING ENERGY AND I DIDN'T KNOW REALLY WHAT IT WAS. WHAT IT ENDED UP BEING WAS THE NEED TO BE AN ARTIST'

LOIS CHILES

(Above) on the left, Thumper (Trina Parks) and Bambi (Lola Larson) in *Diamonds Are Forever*.

Maria Grazia Cucinotta (opposite) played the 'Cigar Girl' in *The World Is Not Enough*, a dangerous and beautiful assassin. She said of her role as a Bond Girl, 'I don't have to kiss him, I just try to kill him.'

The character of the globe-hopping international smuggler, Octopussy on the surface has little in common with actress Maud Adams, but Adams was equally adept at world travel. She lived in Sweden, France, and New York and travelled extensively as a top fashion model before she was in her mid-twenties. Like her character, Adams had strong goals from an early age. An appearance in a Lip Quencher lipstick commercial in the United States prompted the producer of The Christian Licorice Store to call her. Adams seized the opportunity, diving into acting lessons. 'I wanted to be an actress in the fiercest of ways. I really was a very ambitious young lady at the time.'

If there is one actress who seems far more innocent than her on-screen character, it is Lynn-Holly Johnson who plays Bibi Dahl in *For Your Eyes Only*. 'I was thrown into this business pretty much out of luck, having been a competitive figure skater,' Lynn-Holly comments modestly. In fact, she had been performing in front of the camera from a very young age. 'I was Chicago's busiest model by the time I was eight years old,' she admits, 'and I had done 120 commercials by the age of ten.' She won second place in the Novice Level Women's competition in the US Figure Skating Championships at the age of fourteen. Lynn-Holly's natural girlish enthusiasm comes though in her language. "The next thing I knew, Cubby Broccoli wanted to see me for this Bond movie ... it was just kinda neat, y'know. I had no idea what I was getting myself into. And I tell ya, it was the best adventure ever."

Although Carey Lowell (Pam Bouvier in *Licence To Kill*) did not make her feature film debut until she was in her mid-twenties, her background was in perfect tune with a Bond woman. Her father, James Lowell, took his family all over the world. As a result, Carey lived in places as diverse as Holland, France, the US and Libya during her youth. She began modelling after moving to New York in her twenties, being photographed for clients like Calvin Klein and Ralph Lauren as well as most major fashion magazines.

'I left modelling basically because of a film called *Club Paradise*. It was the first film I ever did, and we went to Jamaica for two months and I was surrounded by some of the most talented and funny people I had ever met. I thought, "This is the way to make a living. I would much rather do this."'

'I've been a very lucky girl,' says Michelle Yeoh (Wai Lin in *Tomorrow Never Dies*), arguably the most athletic of the Bond Girls. She entered swimming and diving meets, and even won the title of Malaysian Junior Squash Champion. Her father's success as a barrister and solicitor allowed her to travel to England to study at the age of fifteen. Upon matriculation, she entered the Royal Academy of Dance to study ballet. Returning home for a summer, she discovered that her mother had entered her into the Miss Malaysia beauty pageant without her knowledge. She won the title, representing the country at the Miss World competition.

The title led to an offer to appear in a Hong Kong television commercial for magnate Dickson Poon (whom she later married and subsequently divorced). Poon offered to sign her to appear in movies for his company D&B Films. Yeoh's athletic nature shone through and she soon participated in the signature Hong Kong action scenes. Training extensively, Yeoh often risked her life for her work, and quickly earned a reputation for doing dangerous stunts in films like *Supercop* (1992), gaining legions of loyal fans across the globe.

How to be a Bond Girl

How does an actress end up in a Bond film? There are many paths. Some, like Michelle Yeoh, have the part tailored for them. In developing the script for *Tomorrow Never Dies*, the filmmakers created opportunities to showcase her amazing physical skills. Others, like Gloria Hendry (Rosie Carver in *Live And Let Die*), find themselves swept up in the Bond phenomenon. Hendry, one of the first African-American Playboy Bunnies, had been working in Los Angeles on *Black Caesar* when her New York manager called urging her to return for an interview. 'When I walked in the door, I met Harry Saltzman, this wonderful awesome individual sitting at a desk, in a very soft light … I was really somewhat taken over by his presence, and all I heard him say was "How soon can you fly to New Orleans?" I said, "Anytime." He said "How about in two hours?"

'I'd never been down to New Orleans before in my life. [At the airport] they had the sign up with my name on it, and they picked me up in a limousine. They drove me over to the French Quarter, to a wonderful hotel, and … a fine French restaurant, and Roger came in, and Guy Hamilton [the director] came in, and we're sitting there having dinner.' If it sounds like something out of a Bond movie, it was as close as one can get in real life.

For Lana Wood (younger sister of Natalie), casting came simply at the suggestion of the screenwriter working on *Diamonds Are Forever*. 'It would probably sound a lot better … if I had gone on interviews with 500 other people and beat them all out, but none of that happened,' she says. 'What happened is Tom Mankiewicz, who is a dear friend of mine, said that he was doing this film and he was speaking with Cubby Broccoli and he said, "I've got the perfect girl to play Plenty O'Toole."'

Michelle Yeoh performing her own stunt from *Tomorrow Never Dies*.

Not all casting sessions went so smoothly, particularly on the second Bond film, *From Russia With Love*. After the near magical coup of Ursula Andress in *Dr. No*, Cubby Broccoli and Harry Saltzman decided to see if they could repeat their success at finding an unknown and turning her into a star. Even before *Dr. No* opened in the US, the filmmakers' search garnered headlines in the *Los Angeles Times*, 'Wanted: a Young Greta Garbo'.

The massive talent search was designed to generate publicity, and it included allowing reporter (and future biographer of Cubby Broccoli) Donald Zec into auditions. Zec published the rather harsh conclusions of the filmmakers, which were based almost solely on physique. The hopefuls were deemed too fat, too thin, and too underdeveloped.

The search for a leading lady for *Thunderball* was equally as arduous. An absurd number of actresses vied for the part, including Luciana Paluzzi. 'I tested for the role of Domino … I arrived in London, and there were about a hundred girls, I couldn't believe how many people there were in the make-up room.

'I did the test for the leading role, and then I went back to Rome. And a month went by. Two months went by. I didn't hear anything from anybody. I got a call one day, and Terence said, "I have good news, and I have bad news …" And he said, "Well, the bad news is that you can't play the role of Domino." He said, "The good news is that you're going to play the role of Fiona."'

The filmmakers had cast French actress Claudine Auger for the role of Domino. That change allowed Terence Young to have the red-haired Irish villainess, Fiona Kelly, rewritten as an Italian, now named Fiona Volpe.

There were many major actresses who had a close call with 007. Raquel Welch, Julie Christie, Faye Dunaway and Catherine Deneuve have all been strongly considered for roles, but various factors kept them from becoming Bond Girls.

Luciana Paluzzi (Fiona Volpe in *Thunderball*) became an actress by accident when a friend of her father's came for dinner. The man, an assistant director, complained that director Jean Negulesco could not find an actress for a small part in *Three Coins in the Fountain* (1954). His eyes lit on young Miss Paluzzi, and she soon found herself employed. 'I went on-set and I said, "This is what I want to do the rest of my life."'

Roger Moore (above) poses with Bond Girls from *Octopussy*.
Clockwise from the top: Mary Starin, Carole Ashby, Tina
Robinson, Gillian de Terville, Carolyn Seaward.

Britt Ekland (opposite) on why she wanted to be in a Bond film:
'I'd seen Ursula Andress come out of the sea with the bikini,
and I just thought no one could ever look that fantastic. And,
after having seen that, I always wanted to be a Bond Girl.'

'I WANT TO PLAY MARY GOODNIGHT'

BRITT EKLAND TO 'CUBBY' BROCCOLI

A number of actresses missed their first chance to be in a Bond film, but had a second opportunity. Martine Beswick lost out at a casting call for *Dr. No*, but eventually appeared in two Bonds (*From Russia With Love* as Zora and *Thunderball* as Paula).

Lois Chiles was considered for the role of Anya in *The Spy Who Loved Me* after sitting next to director Lewis Gilbert on a transatlantic flight. Likewise, Carole Bouquet was up for Holly Goodhead, the role Chiles played in *Moonraker*. Bouquet was eventually cast in *For Your Eyes Only*.

Probably the strangest (to be polite) casting gambit came with *A View To A Kill*, when director John Glen was looking to fill the role of Dominique, who performs a show with butterfly marionettes. Actress Carole Ashby, who had already appeared in *Octopussy*, remembers Glen's approach. 'I got a phone call: "Carole, it's John." "John?" I said. "I know a few Johns." "John Glen," he replied. "I'm just at the studio, we're having a chat. Have you got big tits and can you whistle?"'

Carole deemed her bust normal, but informed Glen that she could not whistle. She got the part anyway.

A few Bond Girls lobbied for the chance to be in a Bond film, most notably Britt Ekland, who had been married to Peter Sellers when the actor appeared in the unofficial 007 film, *Casino Royale*. 'When I read that Cubby Broccoli was doing another Bond film,' Ekland says, 'I dressed up the way I thought a secretary should look, with a little white blouse buttoned all the way up, and a little sweater, and I put my hair in a bun in the back, and a long skirt … And I went to his office, and I said, "I want to play Mary Goodnight." And he said, "But you don't understand, the character in the book, we sometimes don't use the whole book. We sometimes just use part of the plot and the names." With that he just sent me back home.

'I went to the States and did another movie, and read in the paper that a Swedish girl called Maud Adams was doing the new Bond film, and I was devastated. Well, as we know, she played the villain's girlfriend. And I came back to London, Cubby called me up and he said, "Could you come and see me?" I went over to his house, and he said, "Here you are." And he put the manuscript in my lap. It was like a dream come true.'

Zena Marshall almost missed her chance to appear in *Dr. No*. She had received a call from a friend of director Terence Young asking if she would be interested in screentesting for the role. Zena showed up only to discover thirty other hopefuls were vying for the role. 'I saw Chinese girls, mostly Oriental women and French girls,' she remembers. Sitting in her dressing room, Marshall realized it was five in the afternoon, so she thought she should see how much longer she should wait. As she entered the stage, she saw the crew were wrapping up for the day. 'Terrence saw me and he said, "my God, we forgot about Zena! We've got to test her."… He walked on to the set and said, "Boys, we've got our own Zena here. We'll have to work much later if we're going to give Zena a chance. Are you willing?" And he looked up at the gantry at all the crew and they all shouted, "Yes, have a go!" I was very touched, it was charming. And I got the part, after all that.'

'THIS PERFUME IS FOR YOU AND THIS IS A CONTRACT TO APPEAR IN THE FIRST JAMES BOND MOVIE'

TERENCE YOUNG TO MARGUERITE LEWARS

When the Bond series began, the filmmakers consciously searched for actresses like Zena Marshall who were at once exotic and accessible. This meant the characters these actresses played had to speak with a voice that was neither pedestrian nor heavily accented. Hence, when it came time to record the dialogue, the directors usually strove to have the Bond women say their lines with a 'mid-Atlantic' accent.

The direction to play the part 'mid-Atlantic' was common among British filmmakers in the Fifties and Sixties. Zena Marshall recalled her first encounter with the term while shooting *Dr. No*. Director Terence Young told her, "'She's Chinese, but you don't really play her Chinese, you play her more international, mid-Atlantic." I said, "What on earth is that?" So, he said, "Well, it's a woman men dream about, but who doesn't really exist.'"

Thus, Honey Ryder comes across as neither Swiss (like Ursula Andress) nor Jamaican. Tatiana Romanova is played with only a hint of a Slavic accent. In *Thunderball*, Domino is meant to be French, but her accent is deliberately light. This sense of international harmony in the acting did not spill over into the casting, at least on one occasion. When West German actress Karin Dor faced a casting dilemma for the role of Helga Brandt on *You Only Live Twice*, she found that Sean Connery was not above a little bit of needling concerning her ability to work in Britain.

'I had the contract, but I did not have the working permit. So we were sitting in the Dorchester Hotel ... waiting for it. Mr Saltzman came and said, "If we don't get the working permit in the next three or four days, we have to pay you out." I would have gotten the money without working.

'That was the year 1966 when the World Cup final was England against West Germany. Sean Connery said, "One thing I want to tell you. If West Germany wins this game, you're never getting your working permit." And I should tell you, we lost the game in extra time. Two days later, I had my working permit.'

Marguerite Lewars (the photographer in *Dr. No*) was originally asked to audition for the part of Miss Taro. She turned it down because it was too risqué for her. 'They had me reading for a part where I was supposed to be wrapped in a towel, lying on a bed, kissing a strange man. I said, "Who is this man I'm supposed to be kissing?" and Terence Young said to me, "This man is Sean Connery." And I said, "I've never heard of him." And he said, "Well you soon will."'

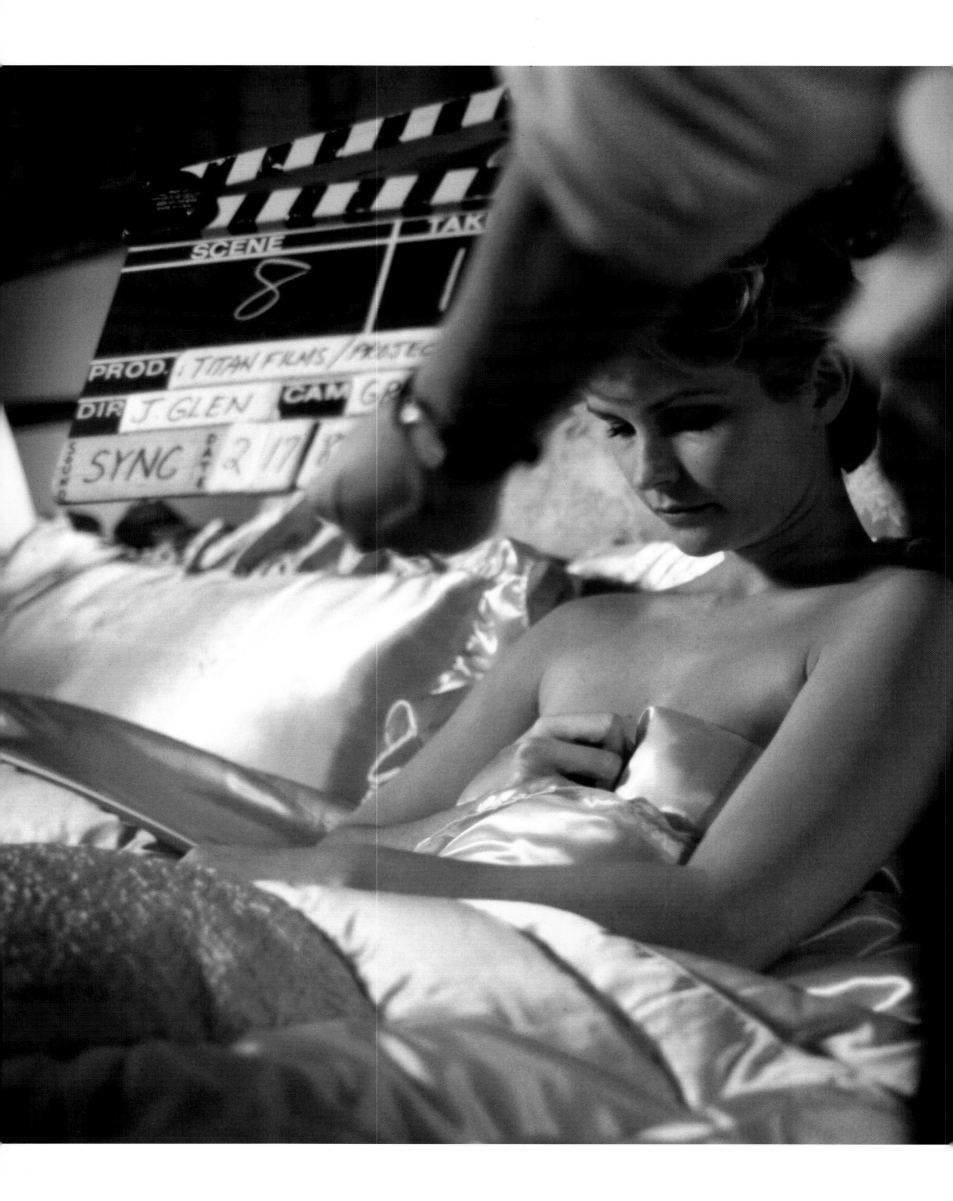

Screentests

In 1961, Sean Connery refused to do a screentest for Bond, so the producers convinced him to help them test actresses for the role. Connery later reported that he knew he was being tested too, but he went along with it. A similar technique was used on two occasions for testing actresses in the Eighties. Maud Adams recalls her casting call for *Octopussy* seemed much more about her co-star than herself. 'I was asked to send current photographs of myself to be looked at for consideration in the new Bond film. I really thought this was very odd ... Shortly thereafter, I was asked if I would go to London and do a screentest. Then I found out that Roger had not signed up for the next Bond and they were considering somebody new.

'So then my reasoning went something like this: obviously, they know me and we get along well, and they probably just want me to be there in order to screentest James Brolin [who was the front-runner for the role of Bond at the time].' When Moore and the producers came to terms, Brolin lost out on the role. Adams did not.

When Moore left 007 for good after *A View To A Kill*, Maryam d'Abo agreed to help test one potential candidate for the role. 'I did it with this lovely actor. We went to [the same] acting school in London.'

After the test, d'Abo worked on a film in Germany set in the 1920s which was never completed. 'Back in London,' d'Abo recalls, 'I bumped into Barbara Broccoli, Cubby's daughter, who was surprised to see how different I looked. Little did I know they were casting *The Living Daylights* when she said, "I must arrange for you to meet Cubby and Michael again."'

Fiona Fullerton played Pola Ivanova in *A View To A Kill*. She also helped the producers in 1986 when they were casting for a new actor to play Bond. 'I turned up one day at the studio in Los Angeles and we tested five different actors, and I got to do a love scene with every single one. It was great.' The opposite photograph shows Fiona during the filming of the Bond screentests.

Shooting Bond

Every Bond actress tells similar stories about the experience of working on an 007 extravaganza. Maud Adams, Luciana Paluzzi, Caroline Munro and many others endorse Lois Chiles's verdict: 'Cubby Broccoli definitely created a family feeling. They treated us so well. It was first class all the way – the best hotels, the best food.'

Talisa Soto, who played Lupe Lamora in *Licence To Kill*, echoed the sentiments of all the actresses discussing Cubby Broccoli. 'He was such a wonderful, sweet man, and it was a pleasure to have known him.' The actresses are equally generous in their praise for the other producers – Harry Saltzman and Michael Wilson, and many count themselves as personal friends of Barbara Broccoli.

Although exotic locales are a part of the Bond universe, often actors shoot most of their material at the studios, as Honor Blackman recounts. 'I was at Pinewood Studios in England. I didn't get further than Northolt Airport with my part. Everybody thinks I had exotic locations. I didn't.'

Likewise, Shirley Eaton never went to Miami Beach to shoot her scenes at the Fontainebleau Hotel. It was all recreated on the stages at Pinewood Studios. Her balcony footage married with shots taken by a small unit months before. Eaton eventually travelled to Miami to promote the film.

'We were supposed to go to Turkey,' Martine Beswick recalls, talking about *From Russia With Love*. 'We had the visas, we had the passports, everything was ready, and at the last minute, they said, "We're going to shoot it on the back lot." We were so disappointed.'

Beswick made up for being studio-bound with her work on *Thunderball*, which involved weeks in Nassau, Bahamas.

Carey Lowell had high hopes for travel when she signed on to the cast of *Licence To Kill*. 'I grew up in Colorado, and Mexico was a place that I had visited frequently before then, so when I heard I got the Bond film, I thought – Morocco, China, you know, India – beautiful exotic places. But they said, we'll be shooting in Mexico City for the duration of the film, which was okay.'

Aside from the film's base at the historic Estudios Churubusco Azteca outside Mexico City, Carey also shot scenes in Key West (which she refers to as 'the T-shirt capital of the world') and on location in Acapulco and at Otomi, a cultural centre built for the indigenous Otomi people of central Mexico.

In *GoldenEye*, neither Famke Janssen nor Izabella Scorupco travelled to Russia, although half the film was set there. Famke went to Monaco while Izabella filmed in Puerto Rico. Halle Berry went to Spain for *Die Another Day*, but, like her co-star Rosamund Pike, never set foot in Iceland, or, for that matter, on the Korean peninsula, where the film's climax was set (but not shot).

Sean Connery and Daniela Bianchi in Istanbul during the shooting of *From Russia With Love*.

Of course, the sets on a Bond film can be just as amazing as any location, particularly, according to Karin Dor, on *You Only Live Twice*. 'Ken Adam, the production designer of the picture, showed me the volcano crater. It was in a big temporary stage of its own. In the whole of Pinewood Studios, there didn't exist such a big stage, so they built the set of the crater first and then built the temporary stage around it. Ken Adam told me they used more steel for building the crater than they used for the Hilton in London. It's unbelievable. It was overwhelming.'

Lois Maxwell's scenes as Moneypenny were almost always shot in the studio, and most of her lines were delivered in close proximity to her desk. She did get to travel to Portugal for *On Her Majesty's Secret Service* for 'about five wonderful days' and worked a day in Dover for *Diamonds Are Forever*. She also had high hopes for *The Spy Who Loved Me*. 'I remember when I read the script I thought, oh, marvellous! I'm going to be in Egypt! But it didn't work at all.' Her office in an ancient temple was built at Pinewood Studios.

Maxwell did go to Paris for her studio work on *Moonraker*, and on to Venice, Italy, for a brief scene. Oddly, the Venice location was doubling for Brazil. Maxwell loved the camaraderie on the set. 'In Venice they had one location which was an old monastery. And we'd have a wonderful time at lunch and exchange ideas and stories and so on. It was just absolutely lovely.'

Lois Chiles also fell in love with Venice. 'It's one of the most romantic cities in the world, and has this wonderful quality of sweet sadness about it. Being there for a month doing the movie was great ... People in the city were so nice to us ...'

Angela Scoular's experiences filming atop a Swiss Alp during the shooting of *On Her Majesty's Secret Service* were equally memorable. 'We had to go up a ski lift every morning for work, and we passed the Eiger and the Jungfrau ... It was quite spectacular. It was the most incredible journey.'

Diana Rigg had a similar reaction to location shooting on the Schilthornbahn for the film, as she told reporter Dick Stroud during shooting. 'It's absolutely enchanting, breathtaking and particularly after the cable car ride, and you get off in this little town, which is situated on a plateau – ridiculously situated. And then you clamber into this horse-drawn carriage because we have no cars. You clip-clop through the streets, very narrow, one street. It's absolutely marvellous.'

Barbara Bach, producer Cubby Broccoli and Roger Moore on Ken Adam's amazing super-tanker set during the filming of *The Spy Who Loved Me*. Barbara Bach left work in front of the cameras and has gone on to help found *The Romanian Angel Appeal* in 1990 as well as performing additional work for other charities.

'I TOTALLY GOT INTO THIS WHOLE VOODOO THING, IT JUST ENVELOPED ME'

JANE SEYMOUR

Out of this world

Location shooting means more than just incredible scenery. The Bond films gave many actresses the chance to explore other cultures, as Jane Seymour recalls. 'Geoffrey [Holder, who played Baron Samedi] took me into the centre of Jamaica, to a voodoo meeting ... And there were all these women dressed in white, and they were dancing, and they were going crazy, slaughtering chickens, and it was amazing, it was scary. Except Geoffrey was great and big and powerful and right next to me. After a very short time I totally got into this whole voodoo thing, it just enveloped me, and I found myself dancing with them. It was very hypnotic. I'm so glad I got to do that, because then I understood what it was [Geoffrey] was trying to recreate. And, obviously, it was an incredible privilege for me to go out there and do that.'

The location that left the strongest emotional impact on the actresses on any particular film was Udaipur, India, in *Octopussy*. Maud Adams describes the dichotomy of poverty and wealth that existed when she arrived there to film. 'It's this humid, hot, hot place and bustling with people everywhere, and there are people sleeping on the street in rolled-up blankets and it's very, very difficult to take.' Kristina Wayborn recalls the strange experience of going out on the streets to shop. 'People wanted to touch us. We found out later it was for good luck.'

'We had lovely times there,' remembers Carole Ashby, one of Octopussy's girls in the film. 'The poverty upset me because there's nothing in the middle. We're in these wonderful exotic hotels and there were these children living and dying on the streets.

'The crew became very friendly with [the locals] and they'd been there for weeks and weeks and looked after children. They were sending money out to them and actually had a tremendous bond, if you don't mind the pun, with the people there.'

'There is a tremendous difference between the rich and the poor,' Maud Adams notes. 'It can be quite shocking when you come with your Western thinking and to all of a sudden be met by this culture and way of life that they have there. But it is also so beautiful, and the people are extraordinary, the culture is so ancient. There are so many wonderful things to take in and absorb that it took years to really

come to grips with all the experiences that I had when I was there.'

Wayborn agrees. 'India was magical for me. I never knew I was going to feel that way about it. It actually had an impact on me for a long time after we left.'

'We stayed in a beautiful place,' says Adams. 'It belonged to the Maharani of Udaipur who had a palace along the lakeside. Part of the palace had been converted into a hotel, and we were the first guests to live in this hotel. It was a beautiful palace with an inner courtyard and it was mostly made of marble and stone ... The courtyard lent itself to wonderful dinners at night ... outside under the stars, where everybody would tell stories.'

The Octopussy girls were housed on the lake in the Lake Palace Hotel where the atmosphere was somewhat different, as Carole Ashby recounts. 'It was great. At night they'd put all the Bond Girls there so that the crew and the other male actors couldn't get to us. But then of course they paid boatmen to get over to us ... and we'd have the most wonderful parties. And I suppose the [male members of the crew] who got lucky stayed over in the rooms. The ones not so lucky were staying on loungers by the swimming pool, and the rest were in the lobby or still hanging around by the boats.'

The stunts

One question asked of the Bond Girls is, 'Did you do your own stunts?' Insurance regulations generally prohibit most actors from performing any seriously dangerous activities, but there seem to be quite a few exceptions in the Bond films.

Performers with specific skills, like Lynn-Holly Johnson, are rarely doubled. 'I did all my own skating, of course, and I did my own skiing.'

Michelle Yeoh, renowned for performing her own stunts in Hong Kong movies, faced restrictions on *Tomorrow Never Dies*, but she quickly worked around them. 'Roger [Spottiswoode, the director] had a good time with that. I'm always saying, "I can do that," and he's like, "I know you can do that, just keep quiet." But by the end of it, we worked around it. With the [close shots of climbing around on the] motorbikes, going down the building, you can see that I'm doing all the physical things ... It's a learning experience for [the Bond film-

Jane Seymour (Solitaire in *Live And Let Die*) with Geoffrey Holder.

makers] as well.' The producers appreciated Yeoh's ability and willingness to undertake dangerous stunts but there was no way they could allow her to perform some of the riskier manoeuvres.

Luciana Paluzzi had to ride a motorcycle for one shot in *Thunderball*. 'They came on the set that morning with this motorcycle, and said, "You have to ride it," and I said, "I've never been on a motorcycle in my life." Someone said, "We'll teach you" ... So we go on the side and for half an hour I'm learning. Then we go to shoot it and I made a mistake. The motorcycle shot forward with such speed that I saw this wall coming. I veered to the left and fell down, and I scraped my leather suit, ripped it, ripped my underwear.

'So I was lying on the floor waiting for somebody to come and get me. And here comes Terence [Young, the director], and I thought that he would say, "Oh, Luciana, what happened to you? Poor baby." Whatever. He starts yelling at me. "Did you see what you did to the motorcycle?"' Luciana laughs at the memory, also describing her director as a 'second father to me'. The scene was ultimately worth it. 'I got off the motorcycle and threw it in the water, and then I take off the helmet and I shake my hair. And my husband Michael says that when he saw the movie, he fell in love with me right that minute. It took him ten years to find me.'

Fight scenes are always a challenge for performers. Kristina Wayborn reportedly let loose with a punch that sent a stuntman to the hospital during the climactic battle in *Octopussy*. In another shot, she was supposed to disarm a stuntman. 'He had a bazooka that weighed probably about seventy pounds, and when I kick it out of his hand they were supposed to change it with a plastic one. Well, [the stuntman] forgot. I actually kicked that seventy-pound bazooka with my bare feet, and broke a couple of little bones in my foot. So I was almost mortally wounded for that last sequence. I was so glad at that point to just be able to kiss Q!'

Tanya Roberts found that her main stunt involved quite a bit of dangling. 'I was doing a lot of hanging – hanging from the burning elevator shaft, hanging from the zeppelin, hanging off the San Francisco bridge, which, of course, we did in front of blue backing in the studio. And then hanging from the ladder of the fire truck in San Francisco ... I'm very athletic and physical, so I don't have problems with that. But the elevator shaft was a little scary, because there was a fire. It wasn't near enough to hurt us, but it still gives you the feeling that you want to get out of the shaft, which was the idea of the scene, so it worked.'

Denise Richards had to make a long underwater swim for the finale of *The World Is Not Enough*. Even though the scene was filmed in a tank at Pinewood Studios, it was still challenging. 'It was the last three weeks of shooting ... We were literally in that tank for three weeks. They had me work with a diver and a respirator beforehand. I'd never been scuba-diving and [safety divers] were swimming underneath me in case anything happened. But it can be scary 'cause that water was a lot stronger than I thought it would be.'

Izabella Scorupco (with Pierce Brosnan in *GoldenEye*) found that running from the train explosion (pictured opposite) was not nearly as scary as being on the set during the collapse of the Severnaya satellite control station.

Surprisingly few women in the Bond films have had to become adept at firing guns like a pro. As a CIA agent, Carey Lowell had to learn the first trick of shooting a gun in a movie. '[Benicio del Toro] was doing some method acting, and I pull out my gun. I start to shoot at him and I'm going – ' Carey blinks and flinches. 'They're saying, "Why are you squinting? Why are you flinching? You fire a gun all the time." ... So I had to go like this – ' she fixes a hard, determined stare ' – and just shoot and keep my eyes open, because you don't flinch when you're a CIA operative shooting a gun.'

Actresses often have to deal with explosions. Izabella Scorupco managed to look good while running from a huge blast in *GoldenEye*, but Britt Ekland had a different experience on *The Man With The Golden Gun*. 'She got thoroughly scared once when she was running away from explosives,' co-star Maud Adams recalls, 'and stumbled and almost didn't get away.'

Britt remembers the details. 'What they do is they set up explosions and you run it through and through. Everything is timed immaculately on the second. It's not a minute, it's just seconds. So, of course, when we shoot it Roger grabs my hand and we start running. The explosions go, and I'm wearing a bikini, and they are very, very close ... One of them went off and ... you're very vulnerable when you're half-naked. I could feel it, and I freaked out. I threw myself on the floor. And you see Roger dragging me up, and that was real.'

Britt, at least, felt she had rehearsed the scene before the explosions. Jane Seymour was not so fortunate. For some reason, the film-makers decided it was safe to allow Jane to take part in some very nerve-wracking stunt work. 'I was in this stunt with the double-decker bus where it goes through the bridge and the top level comes off. Just before I was supposed to do it, I said, "Roger's not doing this?" And they said, "No, no, no, we have a stuntman. He works for the London Bus Company. Maurice Patchett." So I met Maurice, and he looked a lot like Roger, so I thought well, that'll work. Then it suddenly occurred to me, why wasn't there a double for me? So I asked the stuntman, "Do you know if this works? Have you tried it before?" "Oh, no, no, no." ... I was about to walk off the bus, but I was twenty and terrified of Harry Saltzman. And, of course, all the press were there, and Rex Reed, this big journalist, was there. I wanted to come across sort of like a professional. I wanted to get out of that bus so bad, but we went through, and I really thought I was going to die. I mean, we went under that bridge, and nobody knew whether we were going to make it. And when I look at the film, you couldn't tell if it was me or who it was. I mean, thank God I was wearing orange. I don't think you would have seen me at all in any other colour!'

Rosamund Pike, as Miranda Frost in *Die Another Day*, on being cast in a Bond film: 'It's one of the biggest votes of confidence and compliments you can be given. It's one of the coolest gigs you can be offered ... Somehow all these years of films have been crystallized into one idea of a "Bond Girl" – it involves some silhouette and statement of sex appeal – and actually, if you line them all up they'd all be really strong women.'

'I REMEMBER A LOT OF CAMERAMEN ON THE SIDE, ANGLING THEIR CAMERAS I SUPPOSE WAITING TO SEE IF ANYTHING EXTRAORDINARY WOULD HAPPEN'

ZENA MARSHALL ON SHOOTING HER BEDROOM SCENE WITH SEAN CONNERY

The love scenes

The Bond Girls also have the challenge of working with Bond, usually in very close quarters. Often these scenes are shot before the actors get to know each other, and always with at least a few crew members watching. 'It's awkward,' admits Denise Richards. 'Those scenes are always uncomfortable ... It's Bond and it's PG, so it's very tame but still, it's kind of awkward going to work and kissing your co-star. But he's not a bad co-star to be kissing.'

Some actresses are less uncomfortable than others. Honor Blackman obviously enjoyed her embraces with Sean Connery. 'I don't see how you could work with him and not have sparks, or do anything with him and not have sparks,' she says.

Connery's sex appeal to his co-stars was not always evident upon first meeting. When Karin Dor was cast in *You Only Live Twice* she had never seen a Bond film and wasn't familiar with Connery. 'I came over with my agent. She told me about Sean Connery and how women are getting crazy and just flipped over him. I met him, and I thought, "Yeah, he's a nice man." ... He was sitting and rehearsing and I thought, nothing. I said to my agent, "Women are getting crazy over him? I think he's boring!" She said, "I don't understand that either!" Then they said, "Let's shoot." And the clapper fell and all of a sudden there was a sparkle! That was a totally different man! He was fantastic! And I must say, he was a very good colleague.'

Luciana Paluzzi reveals that even the most passionate-looking bedroom scenes are not always what they seem. 'Maybe because I was in bed with Sean, [the publicist] decided to have all these photographers on the set. There must have been easily fifty photographers on the set as we were shooting that scene. They decided that we were going to do the scene for them three times without the

camera rolling so that they could shoot away. And then after that they were thrown out of the set. Aside from that the scene was not very memorable, because we didn't really kiss.'

Zena Marshall's bedroom scene in *Dr. No* was carefully choreographed. 'Sean and I were in bed, together, and he was wearing underpants, all very correct. I was wearing little panties. No bra, but we pinned the sheets on either side very carefully in case something would show ... We spent three days shooting that because, for Ireland, we couldn't be shot together in bed, Ireland being a very Catholic country. So, they had Sean sitting on the bed. I remember a lot of cameramen on the side, angling their cameras I suppose waiting to see if anything extraordinary would happen.'

Daniela Bianchi's famous bedroom scene with Connery in *From Russia With Love* was filled with humour. 'I was very concerned about keeping the sheet tight around me, because underneath I was dressed in a body stocking. Sean, naturally, did everything he could to complicate things. Then Terence made us repeat the scene so many times, maybe because he hoped to create a certain feeling with Sean, since this was one of the first scenes we shot ... It was rather comical.'

Tsai Chin (Ling in *You Only Live Twice*), recalls making sure her scene passed the censors. 'I spent a couple of days with Sean Connery, which can't be a bad thing. I have to say, I taped over everything so that nobody could see anything. And Sean was always teasing me, saying, "I can see you now. I can see you." So I did it in such a way that it looks like I'm totally nude, but you couldn't see very much.'

Jill St John agreed with the positive consensus shared by all of Connery's co-stars. 'Sean Connery was larger than life. He was amazing. And he's a terrific man, you know.'

'THERE WERE A LOT OF FUN GIRLS THERE ... THEY WERE GOOD BUDDIES'

GEORGE LAZENBY ON HIS FEMALE CO-STARS IN SWITZERLAND

Angela Scoular had the most intimate scene with George Lazenby in his sole outing as James Bond. She remembers him as 'good to work with and professional'. Unfortunately for Lazenby, having been designated as a new male sex symbol, the young actresses in Switzerland were eager to tease him. 'He must have had a terrible time,' recalls Scoular with a laugh. 'We used to ring him up in the middle of the night and say, "Ah! What're you doing? Ah! Ah! Ah!"'

The Bond Girls of the Roger Moore era report that he used humour to keep things light on the set. 'Roger loves to tell absolutely filthy jokes,' says Lois Chiles. 'I was a tomboy, and I have brothers, but I'd never heard jokes like this.'

Maud Adams recalls how important Roger's humour was in keeping the set relaxed during the long hours. 'He's a great practical joker, so that really helped a lot. Of course, he loved to play practical jokes on the people who least expected it, or were the most susceptible to them. And I got quite a few of them. A lot of the times they were somewhat risqué.'

Madeline Smith, who plays Miss Caruso at the beginning of *Live And Let Die*, recalled another aspect of performing a bedroom scene with Roger Moore in the early days of his Bond career – his wife. 'I will tell you that his very, very beautiful wife, Luisa, was never far away. She was always sitting, looking very Italian and very, very beautiful, either at the bottom of the bed, or I could always just distinguish her somewhere in the crowd. Always looking very beautiful, always there.'

The most challenging bedroom scene from the Roger Moore years must be when Bond and Goodhead float weightless at the end of *Moonraker*. Lois Chiles says it was not as graceful as it looked. 'That was the most difficult thing to shoot. It was so uncomfortable. We were on wires with little things on underneath. It was just so bizarre. And I didn't like the line. I had to say, "Take me around the world one more time, James." I just didn't like it ... Maybe it was something I didn't understand about that. I think there's some sexual connotation.'

Timothy Dalton brought a different character to the role of Bond. Two of his co-stars, Maryam d'Abo and Carey Lowell, were amused by his macho manner with them. Lowell recalls how he gave her specific instructions on how to kiss him, 'just sort of brush his lips'.

D'Abo remembers, 'I was inexperienced and Tim was very supportive but sometimes he'd boss me around ... especially in the scenes of me trying to steer the cello case down the hill without breaking his neck!'

Lowell agrees. 'I was completely green, too. I didn't know what I was doing when I did Bond. I mean I had done some films, but I really needed some direction and of all people that gave it to me, it was mostly Tim.'

Sometimes the bedroom scenes can get too hot even for Bond. Famke Janssen has one of the few that does not feature 007 himself. Of course, she is killing her bedmate, an admiral. 'The first time we did it was way over the top, and it really became like an S&M scene. I slapped him in the face and all sorts of stuff happened. I actually gave him a big bruise by his ear. It didn't go through the PG rating, so we had to reshoot that scene. They ended up using the reshoots, which I was disappointed in because the character was more revealed in the previous shots.'

'I NEVER THOUGHT OF MYSELF AS A BOND GIRL ... I GOT KILLED TOO EARLY TO BE A REAL BOND GIRL'

TERI HATCHER (*TOMORROW NEVER DIES*)

The actresses who have worked with Pierce Brosnan have played a variety of roles from violent villainess to Oxford professor. Izabella Scorupco had extensive scenes with Brosnan in *GoldenEye*, and she found her co-star down to earth. 'He's a very nice, humble kind of person. And he takes care of everyone. Doesn't matter who you are on the set. He just treats you as if you were his best friend. He's very nice.'

Brosnan and Michelle Yeoh did not share a traditional love scene. Their most flirtatious moment – showering in a Hanoi alleyway – was not open to the press, but it still felt far from intimate. 'That shower scene was actually very difficult because it was done in the streets of Bangkok ... We had zillions of people staring, and we're trying to be cool and the water's splashing. There were no moments. We just wanted to get out of there.'

'We didn't need love scenes to be physical. We were in so many different positions on the bike when we were together, and that was good enough.'

Sophie Marceau is noted for speaking in abstract terms, and this was certainly the case in some of her interviews conducted in English. It is her 'incredible aloofness and reserve' – as Pierce Brosnan put it – that makes her bedroom scenes in *The World Is Not Enough* so fascinating. Unlike many other Bond Girls, she was surprised by the filmmakers' concern about the possibility of accidentally showing her bare breasts. Coming from France where nudity does not affect the censor ratings she mentioned in interviews that nude scenes did not bother her. 'I'll tell you a secret. It is something actresses need to go through, and I think they look forward to being naked in a movie.'

Rosamund Pike, who had never done a feature film before, told a BBC journalist that her love scene with Brosnan in *Die Another Day* was hairy, but not in the way one might think. 'I always feel a responsibility towards these things, not to dispel myths, but when you do a love scene you tend to wear what they call "modesty panels". They use tape to tape these things to you, and Pierce and I have this scene where we're in this ice swan and there were a lot of furs around. We pulled away after the scene and I looked down to check the tapes and there were these hairs sticking out. I thought, "Oh my God, I'm pulling off Pierce's chest hair!" And then, of course, I realized it was just the kind of teddy bear fur they'd used for the blankets. I was trying to make sure he didn't see.'

Halle Berry's sex scene with Brosnan proved to be the most dangerous to appear in a Bond film.

'I'm cutting a fig in a love scene and it gets lodged in my throat,' Berry told Mary Hart of *Entertainment Tonight*. 'I mean I literally could get no air – and Pierce right away jumps up behind me, hits me, and out comes the fig.'

Pierce Brosnan certainly didn't mind saving Berry. He told *Vogue's* Jonathan Van Meter, 'I have a lot of time for that woman. She's fascinating. She's got great soul and humility, and she knows what suffering is. She knows what it is to have to fight and to be on the outside, and I think that brings a grace and a humour that are sometimes lacking in people who have so much beauty and talent.'

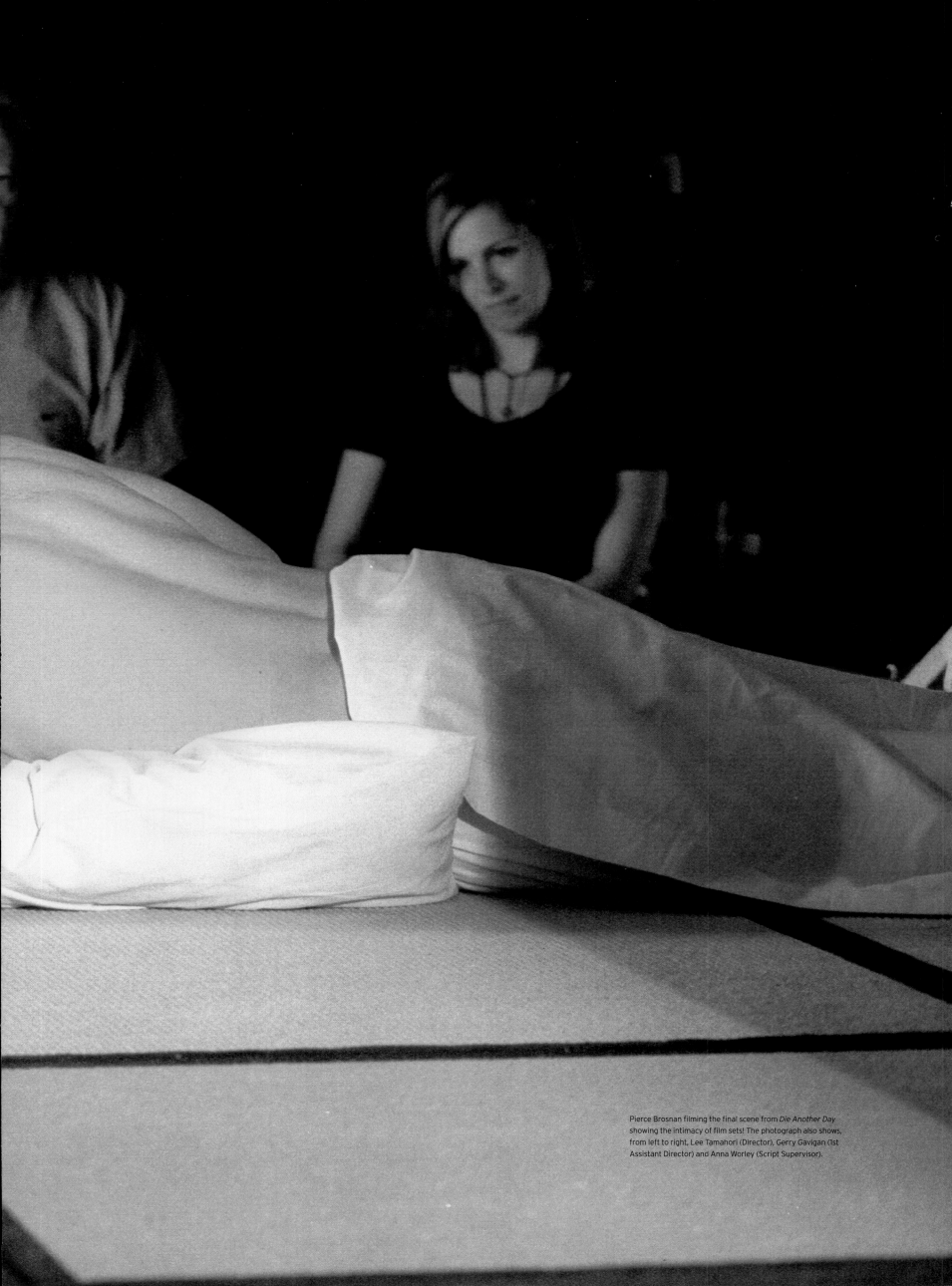

Pierce Brosnan filming the final scene from *Die Another Day* showing the intimacy of film sets! The photograph also shows, from left to right, Lee Tamahori (Director), Gerry Gavigan (1st Assistant Director) and Anna Worley (Script Supervisor).

LIFE

A MATTER FOR
JAMES BOND

Shirley Eaton, gilded victim
in **GOLDFINGER,** funniest
and money-makingest
of the 007 movies

4 THE IMPACT

To be a Bond Girl is like living a Cinderella story. From the moment the filmmakers announce your casting, you are fêted, celebrated, and whisked off on a whirlwind of adventure, complete with beautiful gowns, exotic settings, and a Prince Charming as a co-star.

There are a few important twists. When the clock strikes midnight, you return to the life of a working actress. And, unlike in Cinderella, there is no anonymity when the party's over. There seems to be an expectation within the media that once you have been a Bond Girl, you are labelled a Bond Girl forever.

When I was cast, publicist Jerry Juroe said to me, 'Maryam, can you live with the fact that you will be recognized and get fan mail for being a Bond woman until you die?' I laughed at his comment and replied, 'Jerry, people will forget.' I couldn't think longer than six months in those days, but Jerry was right.

When *The Living Daylights* ended, I came to Hollywood. I felt an unspoken challenge from filmmakers, as if they were saying, 'She's a Bond Girl, but can she act?'

There was a moment when I thought to myself, I'm never going to be able to get away from the Bond Girl image. I remember a few years after *The Living Daylights*, I wanted to audition for a Chekhov play in London. The producer would not let me read for the part. She said that she didn't want a Bond Girl on stage. Moments like that made me want to fight back. What was wrong with being glamorous and beautiful?

As the years passed, I realized that for me, being a Bond Girl was about celebrating my femininity. It was about being independent enough to stand alongside James Bond and all his history. It was also about being secure enough in who I was and enjoying the label of being a Bond Girl with the likes of Honor Blackman, Ursula Andress, Dame Diana Rigg, Famke Janssen, Michelle Yeoh, Halle Berry, and dozens of other wonderful actresses. It's not a bad group to be among. In fact, it is hard to think of another sorority of acting talent of which I would rather be a part.

Maryam d'Abo

Loomis Dean's famous photo of a gilded Shirley Eaton perfectly captured the decadent eroticism hinted at in the film and Fleming's novel. Dean performed extensive on-set photography for the filmmakers on both *Goldfinger* and *Thunderball*. He also took some of the most memorable images to ever appear in *Life* magazine, and original prints of his work have become highly collectable.

Thursday, July 27, 1978

Watched 20/20 [a US news magazine show] and instead of saying, 'In the future everyone will be famous for fifteen minutes,' it was so funny to hear Hugh Downs say, 'As Andy Warhol once said, in fifteen minutes everybody will be famous.' People on TV always get some part wrong, like – 'In the future fifteen people will be famous.'

(The Diaries of Andy Warhol)

THE MEDIA'S INSATIABLE appetite for celebrity has afforded many people their fifteen minutes of fame. Driven by a film's need for publicity, actresses, actors, and directors are thrust at reporters to get maximum media exposure surrounding a film's opening. The goal for a film studio is to create a groundswell of interest in a movie. For an actress, it is to create an audience for this film and her future performances. All too quickly, those who glitter in the media today are forgotten tomorrow. Their fifteen minutes have run out.

Even those who attain prominence in entertainment often fade from memory. Strolling down Hollywood Boulevard's Walk of Fame few will recognize many of the older names from the early days of the film industry. Past generations are forgotten. Close your eyes and try to picture Louise Rainer's face. Drawing a blank? Rainer won back-to-back Oscars for Best Actress in the Thirties. We do remember Rainer's contemporaries. Everyone instantly recalls the image of Walt Disney's Snow White, Greta Garbo's luminous beauty and Marlene Dietrich's sultry bedroom eyes.

Maybe Warhol was also right when he joked, 'in the future fifteen people will be famous'. The Bond Girls have found that enduring fame in the world of film is not based solely on talent nor a rush of publicity during a film's opening. The James Bond films have had tremendous success in creating memories that last, and some of those that last the longest have been created by the Bond Girls.

The Bond actresses have gone through the process of publicizing the films – a process almost as involved as making the movie itself. After their experience with 007, several have found Bond was a launching pad for fulfilling careers. Others have retired to family life or to pursue another career. Some other actresses had film careers that did not blossom after their turn as a Bond Girl. But all have found that being a Bond Girl has remained a larger part of their lives than they imagined.

Maryam d'Abo: 'When we arrived in Vienna I experienced my first big press conference. It was like being in a Bond movie!'

Any actress will tell you it is a unique experience working on a James Bond film, and there is nothing like the media attention 007 generates. In 1962, when Cubby Broccoli and Harry Saltzman started to shoot *Dr. No*, the level of publicity on that film could not be compared to the attention the later films recieved. The film garnered stories in most of the British press and in the *New York Times* even before it completed shooting. *Dr. No* was not, as some have maintained, some little film that nonetheless became a success. The film's lavish premiere in London drew luminaries like W. Somerset Maugham and the world's richest man, J. Paul Getty. It was – in relation to its budget and little known cast – well-publicized on both sides of the Atlantic. Still, no one – not the studio, nor the media – quite knew what they had on their hands with James Bond, as can be seen by one of the earliest publicity appearances by a Bond Girl when United Artists asked actress Zena Marshall (*Dr. No*'s Miss Taro) to accompany Sean Connery to a greyhound racetrack to present the winners cup!

Even before a frame of film was shot on the second Bond movie, *From Russia with Love*, the producers invited the London press to meet the new Bond Girl, Daniela Bianchi, at the Connaught Hotel. Daniela was far from overwhelmed by the dozen photographers that showed up. 'This was the second film, so this character of James Bond still wasn't very well known,' she explains.

By the film's premiere, the scope and scale of the Bond phenomenon had obviously grown. 'First of all they had a poster on Piccadilly Circus that was about six stories high,' remembers Aliza Gur (Vida). 'Never have I seen that much of a crowd. I remember it took one hour for the limo to make its way through.' It had only taken a year, but the life of a Bond Girl had come a long way.

Another year later, Shirley Eaton (Jill Masterson in *Goldfinger*) appeared on the cover of *Life* magazine in the US and a full-colour page in the Sunday supplement of the UK's *Observer*. Still, she wasn't pleased with her billing on the Bond film. She sued, settled, and was soon off on a first-class promotional tour of the US. 'It was kind of madness,' Eaton says. 'Three weeks. A different city every two days.

Every time I got off the plane and saw the press I had a different gold outfit on. It was Chicago, Washington, Los Angeles, everywhere. You have interviews for lunch, and you have interviews for breakfast, and you have interviews for tea, and you have interviews for dinner, so it's a bit hellish, actually.'

The filmmakers employed Honor Blackman to launch a series of premieres across England, and later there was more publicity work in America. She was surrounded daily by swarming reporters and photographers. 'One has to admit it was exciting. It was a great experience for me because I'd done lots of publicity before then, but I wasn't accustomed to what happened in America when you fly from town to town and they open the door and there are 140 journalists there. And each one of them wants an individual interview.'

Honor Blackman did a tremendous job capitalizing on her strong image in the film. '*Goldfinger* did up the ante as far as my career was concerned,' she confesses. 'And I did become very well known. All sorts of things come out of a successful picture.' One of those was a chance to record an album, *Everything I've Got* (which contains the famed camp classic single, a duet with Patrick Macnee, 'Kinky Boots'). A flying school offered her free lessons when the press reported Blackman wasn't a real pilot. 'Just as I was getting near my solo I got a film in Hollywood, and I had to go out there for some months. The moment I came back, one of my adopted children arrived. And, so, life changed entirely and I never finished it.'

Additionally, Blackman went on to publish a book on judo manoeuvres (authored by stuntmen Joe and Doug Robinson), marketed primarily to women. The book flyleaf copy says it all: 'In *Honor Blackman's Book of Self-Defence*, the beautiful motion picture actress who first stunned American audiences – and James Bond – in the film *Goldfinger*, gives away the secrets of her success with men. Or rather her success at holding them in line when they fail to see the line.'

Margaret Nolan (Dink) received publicity by announcing to the London press that Shirley Eaton was not the film's only Golden Girl. Nolan's gilt body appeared in the film's credits and on the poster. That story earned a few inches of text in the tabloids.

With the success of *Goldfinger*, Blackman came to Hollywood. She made three films released in 1965 (*Moment To Moment*, *The Secret of My Success*, and *Life At the Top*), but then left film for two years to raise her children. When Blackman returned, she again teamed with Sean Connery in the Western, *Shalako* (1968).

'I THINK THE PRESSURE BROUGHT ON ONCE AN ACTRESS IS SIGNED TO THE PART IS ENORMOUS. I DON'T THINK ANY OF THE GIRLS EVER HAD ANY IDEA WHAT IT WOULD BE LIKE'

DANA BROCCOLI

Even with the coverage of the *Goldfinger* actresses in full swing, the press began speculating about who would be the new 'Bond babes' in the next film. Six months later, planeloads of journalists from around the world travelled to Nassau to cover *Thunderball*, eager to feed the public's seemingly insatiable appetite for all things 007. 'They chartered two planes that came down with two hundred journalists, and they were on the set for a week every day,' says Luciana Paluzzi (Fiona Volpe). 'I was on the cover of every magazine in Italy, and then in France, and then it was like a boom. You could not pay for it. If you said, "Okay, I want to invest a million dollars in publicity for myself," you couldn't have done it. It was just an incredible overnight exposure.'

'We ended up with *Cosmopolitan*, *Life*, *Look*. After a while it was part of the job,' recalls Martine Beswick (Paula). 'It was pretty amazing.'

Mollie Peters (Patricia in *Thunderball*), who did not film in Nassau, was still stunned by suddenly being elevated to the status of icon. 'The publicity angle had quite an impact … There was a lot of publicity connected with premieres, or fundraising, going abroad, too, to Brazil, and Vienna. Brazil [where she travelled with Martine Beswick] was an eye-opener for me … I was blonde, and I had a tan, I wore a white dress, people wanted to touch me, I found that very strange, and I think it was because of the different colouring, I don't know. Or perhaps in their eyes I'd become something unattainable to them. I don't know what it was, but I found it very difficult to cope with.'

'That actually put it in my face, about fans and how scary it was,' Martine remembers. 'Before it was a lark. We were working as actors, but the publicity was really a lot of fun. When we went to Brazil, I remember Mollie and I had two hours of our own, so we trotted off to the beach. No sooner did we lie down than we were surrounded by these young men. And we thought, "Oh, God, what are we going to do now?" We were very close to the hotel so we managed to get back before they got us.

'Going to the premiere in the evening, they literally attacked and rocked the car and almost broke the windows, screaming, "Bond Girl! Bond Girl!" and it was like really, really scary.'

The mania the actresses experienced surrounding the filming and release of *Thunderball* would set the tone for the experience of being a Bond Girl for the next forty years. On the one hand the films offered unparalleled publicity and visibility. On the other, no actor, male or female, is as big as the character of Bond. To be a Bond Girl meant an actress would 'become something unattainable' as Mollie Peters put it. She had become part of the Bond mythology, elevated to the status of an icon. Many Bond Girls quickly discovered that there aren't that many parts written for icons.

'When I went back to Italy [after doing *Thunderball*],' Luciana Paluzzi recalls, 'the directors – the Fellinis, the Antonionis, the Viscontis – they didn't want to have anything to do with me. They loved me. I knew them all, and they were all very sweet and very nice, but when it came to doing one of their pictures, "No."'

Paluzzi went on to appear in over thirty films before retiring from acting at the end of the Seventies. Her complaint was not lack of work, but the kind of work she was offered. 'I never really got a chance, all through my career, to do something really serious and really satisfying as an actress. I did a lot of things, but they were all commercial.'

Martine Beswick agrees. 'There's two sides to being a Bond Girl. One is really fun and really great. It put me on the map as an actress. But there is always a taint of being a Bond Girl because you don't really do much else afterwards. There are only a few that have gone on … A lot of the women who have been Bond Girls have had to deal with this. It's sort of a bit of the bane of my existence, actually. It's a two-edged sword.' Beswick reflects for a moment. 'I wouldn't change it though, I must say.'

Luciana Paluzzi (Fiona Volpe in *Thunderball*) poses for a publicity photograph in Nassau, the Bahamas.

Life after Bond

The Bond filmmakers find the media assertion that Bond Girls rarely go on to bigger and better things irritating and presumptuous. Producer Barbara Broccoli addresses it directly. 'How many hundreds of movies get released every year where actresses are put in a leading role but are not remembered? In Bond movies, because it is a series, actresses get instant recognition and if they do not remain in the limelight it is perceived that being a Bond woman has hurt their career.'

Obviously, this isn't true. Ursula Andress was deluged with offers for well over twenty years after *Dr. No*. She chose to avoid big, dramatic roles, preferring parts where she would not have to portray complex emotions. Zena Marshall married soon after the film and retired. Daniela Bianchi made a brief attempt to take Hollywood in 1964, but the language barrier proved difficult to overcome. She returned to Italy, starred in over a dozen films in five years, and retired when she married in the late Sixties. In contrast, Honor Blackman's star was still shining brightly in 1990. She secured one of the leading roles in *The Upper Hand*, a sitcom based on the US television show, *Who's the Boss?*. Claudine Auger worked steadily in European films and television movies for decades. Jacqueline Bisset won a minor role in the non-EON Bond spoof *Casino Royale*, but within two years she was co-starring with Frank Sinatra and Steve McQueen. Her career has continued with numerous critical and commercial successes, including the acclaimed television production of *Joan of Arc* in 1999. Although Mie Hama and Akiko Wakabayashi both retired from acting in the Sixties, Hama became a well-known television personality in Japan for many years. Dame Diana Rigg is acknowledged as one of Britain's best actresses over thirty years after her starring role in *On Her Majesty's Secret Service*. Joanna Lumley, who appeared briefly in *On Her Majesty's Secret Service* achieved stardom with the television series *The New Avengers* and *Absolutely Fabulous*. She has also won acclaim for her television documentaries.

While a percentage of the Bond Girls of the Sixties did not find lasting success in high-profile films, a remarkable number worked steadily in lesser-remembered movies or on television. This is the case with the Bond Girls of each decade. Jill St John had a diverse career long before *Diamonds Are Forever*. Nevertheless she felt the role helped her. 'It was great because I got offered a lot of films. As a matter of fact, I was out of work for about a week before I started doing another one. And I did a very, very serious drama after that [*Sitting Targets*], so it was a good contrast.' She successfully negotiated the delicate period between appearing as a Bond Girl and taking on more mature media appearances and acting roles, including becoming an on-air gourmet for a US morning news show, *Good Morning America*.

Caroline Munro also found the benefits of her role in *The Spy Who Loved Me* outweighed the negatives. 'There is a stigma. Once a Bond woman, always a Bond woman. But I don't think that's a bad thing ... It's up to you what you do with that. It opens a lot of doors. It opens them because you've got a little bit of a name. And with that name, yes, they offer you similar parts, but also, out of the similar parts come other parts.'

During the New York publicity for *The Spy Who Loved Me*, producer Cubby Broccoli urged her to take full advantage of the film's visibility. 'Cubby said, "You must stay in America. I can introduce you to people when the Bond film comes out. I know you could work a lot." But I chose to stay at home in England. That's my home and my family's there, so that was my choice. But I was able to work in Europe, which is nice and close for me, and I did some interesting parts over there.'

Caroline Munro (Naomi in *The Spy Who Loved Me*) recalls how she was cast: 'I was doing a campaign in England for Lamb's Navy Rum, and the character that I portrayed in the posters was quite a strong character. I wore a wetsuit, and I carried a knife. Cubby Broccoli saw this image and he said, "Send her to my office." So I went to see him. And I did a screentest, and I got the part.'

Jane Seymour became a major star after moving from London to Los Angeles, for a while unofficially dubbed 'the Queen of the Mini-Series' in the US, and later starring as *Dr Quinn, Medicine Woman*. Seymour's high-profile success does not diminish the work of the other Bond actresses of the decade, but it illustrates the level of accomplishment an actress must receive to get credit for work beyond Bond.

'I wasn't unknown. I'd done a bunch of Shakespearean theatre and stuff like that,' Seymour says. 'There was a stigma attached to it for me for a while, because they wanted to call me a "Bond Girl", and I was absolutely determined to be what I'd originally planned to be, which was a serious actress, a classical actress. So, I think a lot of people thought it was odd that I would choose to go and work in the theatre for about a year. But I've always been pretty proud of [*Live And Let Die*], actually. Especially now. There is nothing cooler than being able to walk around and have young kids come up to you and say, hey, I saw your movie. It's great. And you go, I wonder what movie that was? It wasn't *Dr Quinn*. And then they say, "No, *Live and Let Die*".'

Maud Adams — whose fame outside of her native Sweden is almost entirely associated with her dual starring roles in Bond films — also feels the label of a 'Bond curse' is unfair. 'The press likes to perpetuate the myth that the Bond Girls are beautiful, but they really are only that. And I think it's not true, because most of the girls that have played in the Bond series have continued their careers in the business.'

Adams went through the hoopla of starring in a Bond film twice, the second time after a nine-year gap. When she returned to play Miss Octopussy, she had the advantage of knowing that the publicity surrounding James Bond is different from other films. On *The Man with the Golden Gun*, she had no clue. Adams arrived in Hong Kong before shooting for a start of production press conference. 'I thought it would be a nice one-on-one situation, and I walked into this ball-room with a horde of people and cameras running, and we're all sitting on a dais and being interviewed. That gave me the first indication of what I was in for ... I didn't expect press from all over the world to be so interested in a film that hadn't even been made.'

Jane Seymour came to Hollywood shortly after *Live And Let Die*, but was soured after a producer made an inappropriate advance. She returned to England and 'gave up acting, quit showbiz, and became a full-time housewife.' Fortunately, she was offered a role in Ibsen's *A Doll's House* on the stage and, having returned to the US in 1976, quickly rebuilt her career.

Lois Chiles (Holly Goodhead in *Moonraker*) had a nearly identical experience when she attended the film's press announcement in Paris. 'There were so many photographers everywhere. And it begins to dawn on you that this is bigger than anything you've ever been in before.'

Adams, like Shirley Eaton a decade earlier, learned how draining publicity can become. 'Those promotional tours, they're so full of interviews every single day. I remember how hard they are because you go from city to city and, after a while, you don't know what city you're in. You talk to so many different people and you have no idea who they are. You repeat yourself so often that in the end, you feel really hollow. They're very, very difficult to do because when you've said the same thing so many times you come home in the evening and say, "My God. Who am I?"'

Adams repeats a familiar refrain of the actresses. 'I never expected so much media attention. Certainly, I thought that it would be exciting for a short period of time when the movie came out. I didn't realize how it would be part of my life for the rest of my life. At times it was difficult because I wanted also to be remembered for other work that I'd done. On the other hand, now that I look back on it, I feel really blessed by it because it's kept me alive, in a way that no other movie probably ever could.'

Adams' co-star in *The Man With The Golden Gun* had a similar experience. Britt Ekland spent years resenting that she was never able to capitalize on being in a Bond film. Time and perspective changed that. 'It's like being part of a legend in a way. I think the image of Bond will never go away, and I'm very proud and very pleased when people say, "Oh, you were a Bond Girl." It's not something I look down on, or feel it's a tag I have to carry with me. It's just that was a part of my life then, and it was a great experience.'

Lois Chiles also had a time of adjustment to come to terms with her experience, particularly when she faced hostile questions from reporters about how feminists perceived women in the Bond films. 'In 1979, it was a funny time to be a Bond Girl ... because, at that time, women were protesting their image in the movies, how they had been portrayed. It was a conflicted time to be a Bond Girl.'

She was quoted at the time of the film's release as saying, 'I knew that whatever else the role might require that I bare, it would not be my soul.' The problem was Chiles never made that comment, it was a quote given by a film publicist and then attributed to her. 'I wish I'd had Roger's wit, because I would have handled the press differently, but at the time I was just sort of insulted. I would be sometimes insulted by some of the things Roger would say. I was being a proper feminist at that time, taking myself very seriously.

'But now, it's very fashionable to be a Bond Girl. I'm very proud to have been a Bond Girl, to be a part of it ... it was really interesting, too, to be the lady of that moment.'

Roger Moore and Britt Ekland share a laugh and some milk on the set of *The Man With The Golden Gun*. Shooting cinema commercials for the United Kingdom Milk Marketing Board was one of the many side duties of being in a Bond film in the early Seventies.

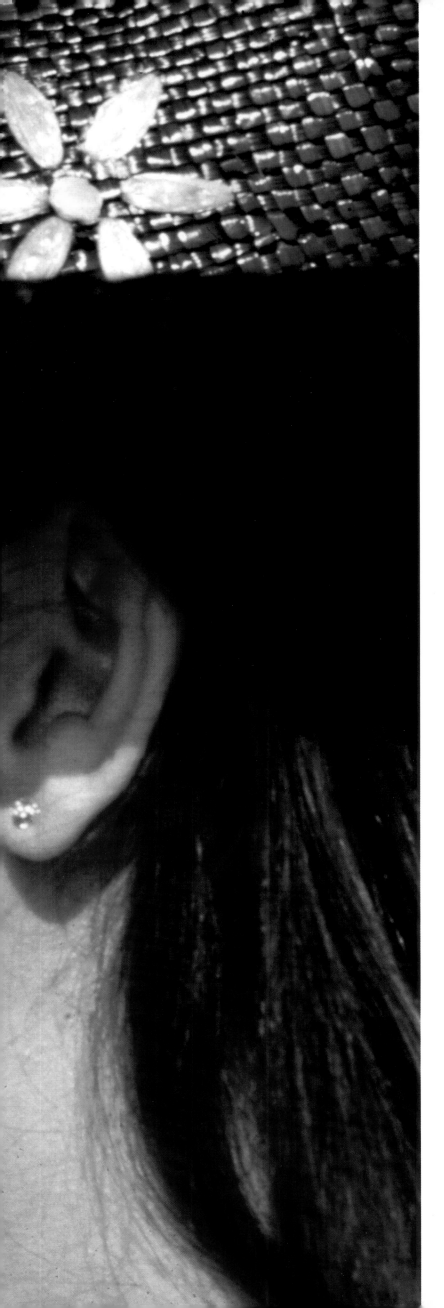

As the Eighties began, the filmmakers found themselves faced with actresses who were not as willing to be presented to the media in the same fashion as Lois Chiles. Carole Bouquet – who was recommended for her part by publicist Jerry Juroe – found similar frustrations on *For Your Eyes Only*, but her tensions bubbled over into interviews. She eagerly told one and all, 'I'm not a sex symbol ... I'm not just another plastic doll.' When asked by a reporter on location in Corfu about Roger Moore's sex appeal, Bouquet made it clear that their age difference did not allow for any chance of a thrill.

Bouquet's comments highlighted the double standard within Bond's public image at a time of mounting awareness of women's issues. On the one hand, the character of Bond needs to be presented as the über-virile irresistible male. On the other hand, actresses were tired of being portrayed as ever-willing sex toys, cooing for the stud-du-jour, and not just in the Bond films. Bouquet's comments echoed a new tone from many actresses of the era, a tone that was openly dismissive of the male-oriented sexuality portrayed in films and on television.

There were many ironies that could not be appreciated at the time. First was that Bouquet's character was anything but overly sexualized. Creatively (as is detailed elsewhere) the film strove to move away from the image of Bond as a spy who simply uses women. Second was that Roger Moore often pleaded with Cubby Broccoli to cast more mature-looking actresses because he had no illusions about the age differences.

Bouquet, who is arguably one of the most beautiful women of her generation, went on to become the face for *Chanel* and has had a tremendously successful acting career in France.

Carole Bouquet did not participate in much of the press surrounding the release of *For Your Eyes Only*. She later appeared in *Nemo* (1984) with Sean Connery's son, Jason. Her next English-language film was *New York Stories* (1989), but in between she appeared in over a dozen European productions.

Cassandra Harris with her husband Pierce Brosnan at the premiere of
For Your Eyes Only (above). When Harris and Brosnan came to Los
Angeles, they had dinner with producer Cubby Broccoli and his wife
Dana. Brosnan later said that on the drive back, he kept repeating,
'The name's Bond, James Bond.'

The filmmakers were baffled by the so-called controversy over the US
poster for *For Your Eyes Only* (opposite). They felt the image showed a
powerful yet sexy woman. In fact, the image was far less sexually
graphic than the posters for many spy films of the Sixties.

Ever since *Dr. No*, shots of Bond surrounded by women had been
powerful publicity tools. For *The Spy Who Loved Me*, one still of Bond
in the midst of a group of decidedly European-looking 'Arab beauties' captured a certain debonair attitude present in Roger Moore's
self-amused approach to the role. For *Moonraker*, Moore was again
surrounded, this time by Drax's 'perfect race' ... or at least the female
members. On *For Your Eyes Only*, Moore posed with 'the Pool Girls'
during the first few days of shooting on Corfu, Greece. Many of these
women, mostly models, also posed for *Playboy* and other publica-
tions. Some even went on international tours to promote the film.
Regardless, their names did not end up in the final credits. They did,
however, receive pages of coverage in the production notes given
out by the studio, including a helpful listing of their measurements
just in case some reporter wanted to buy them an outfit.

One of the women pictured with Roger Moore was listed as a 'tall
English lovely' who 'stands an impressive six feet'. Her name was
listed as Tula, but her legal name was Caroline Cossey. In actual fact
Cossey had been born Barry Cossey and had undergone sex-change
surgery. The *News of the World* uncovered Cossey's true identity
soon after the film's release. The worldwide press had a field day
mocking Bond and *Playboy* for utilizing a transsexual, and Cossey's
old acquaintances were variously trotted out to expose a life left
behind. However personally tragic Caroline's exposure was, the
result of the tabloid coverage brought about an in-depth and public
discussion of transsexual issues. *Playboy* decided not to back away
from its judgment of Cossey's beauty and featured a new pictorial of
the actress. Cossey's public exposure led her to write a book, *Tula: I
Am a Woman*, and she later brought a high-profile legal action
against the British Government to allow transsexuals the right to
marry (the action failed on appeal to the European Court for Human
Rights). She wrote a second book, *My Story*, in 1991.

The US ad campaign for *For Your Eyes Only* stirred up problems.
Some felt the bikini-clad legs showed a bit too much cheek at the
top. Over one-hundred newspapers insisted on altering the bikini line
on the woman. Various models claimed to be the ones posing for the
poster. It turned out to be a composite of two models – Joyce Bartel

provided the legs, but Jane Sumner's arm held the crossbow. *People*
magazine covered the mystery in detail, but received the following
letter in response:

> *What is controversial about the new James Bond ad is not whose
> 'glamorous gams' are depicted but the dangerous message
> being conveyed. For years commercials have shown women as
> sex objects, but this one, with a fully dressed James Bond aiming
> a gun at the crotch of a female whose only identity is her legs
> and buttocks, eroticizes violence. It is no wonder violent crimes
> against women have reached endemic proportions.*
> Stacy Taylor, *Women Against Pornography*

As Lois Chiles noted, it was a conflicted time to be a Bond Girl.

One actress in *For Your Eyes Only* had a tremendously positive
impact on the future of James Bond. Cassandra Harris did not
participate in too much of the media coverage for the film, but she
did strike up a friendship with Cubby Broccoli, which led Cubby to
meet Harris's husband, Pierce Brosnan. Harris tragically died of
ovarian cancer in 1991. She reportedly always thought Pierce should
play Bond, championing him when the role was offered in 1986
(Brosnan was forced to withdraw because of a renewal of his
contract for the US television series, *Remington Steele*). Although
she never saw Brosnan play Bond, she certainly helped illuminate
the path that brought him to the role.

The Bond Girls of the Eighties all had to cope with the shifting and
uncertain image of women in films, and for many in the media, Bond
seemed to be a clear example of an outdated approach. Kristina
Wayborn felt that conflict but she did not let it slow her down. 'It's a
double-edged sword, because glamour is not always popular in some
cases. But for me, it was great, because it's part of film history. I don't
know that it necessarily helps or hurts anybody's career.'

Tanya Roberts told *TV Guide* in 1999 that she did not blame
Bond for any slowdown in her career after *A View To A Kill*. But
subsequently she went on to a successful run in the US sitcom, *That
70s Show*.

'IT'S A DOUBLE-EDGED SWORD ... FOR ME, IT WAS GREAT, BECAUSE IT'S PART OF FILM HISTORY'

KRISTINA WAYBORN (MISS MAGDA IN *OCTOPUSSY*)

For Fiona Fullerton (Pola Ivanova in *A View to a Kill*), the Bond movies gave her a chance to alter her image. She gained fame as a Victorian beauty in *Nicholas and Alexandra* (1971) and John Barry's musical, *Alice's Adventures in Wonderland* (1972). 'My career changed quite dramatically because for the first time ever I was seen as, well, a sex symbol I suppose, as a *femme fatale*. And I had hitherto never been cast in that way before, so it did open lots of doors for me.'

When Timothy Dalton took over the role in 1987's *The Living Daylights*, the films strengthened their focus on the female characters. Nonetheless, the actresses of the Dalton era had to make the choice of how much they wanted to embrace the overall sexy image of the Bond Girls. Part of that image was created through *Playboy* and other men's magazines that featured pictorials of women associated with Bond films.

Jerry Juroe, the long-time publicist for the Bond films, said that the filmmakers enjoyed a strong relationship with *Playboy*, but they never required the actresses to pose. Those choices were always up to the performer and the filmmakers never became directly involved in those negotiations. That said, if an actress was willing to pose, the publicity department would leap in with both feet to help any way it could. Since *Playboy* published The James Bond Girls pictorial in the November 1965 issue, the magazine had covered most of the Bond films with pictorials. *Casino Royale, You Only Live Twice, Diamonds Are Forever, Live and Let Die, The Spy Who Loved Me, Moonraker, For Your Eyes Only, and Never Say Never Again* all received coverage. In both *On Her Majesty's Secret Service* and *Diamonds Are Forever* there are references to *Playboy* in the films themselves. Part of the attraction of the Bond Girls remains the sexual confidence, and these pictorials complemented that aspect of the on-screen imagery. Over the years stars like Ursula Andress, Barbara Bach, Kim Basinger and Tanya Roberts appeared in *Playboy*. Others, like Lois Chiles and Caroline Munro, declined. Munro, for one, now says she wishes she had given it more thought before saying no.

With 1987 marking the 25th anniversary of the Bond films, *Playboy* approached star Maryam d'Abo about appearing in a special layout for the magazine. Because of the longstanding relationship between the magazine and Bond, she ended up making a decision with which she was ultimately not comfortable. 'It was an expectation and then I got seduced,' d'Abo says. 'They said, "Oh, but you will get the best photographer you want. They'll be really interesting shots in the French style."

'I requested Terry O'Neill. And he pulled out at the last minute. Then I ended up with this other photographer [long-time *Playboy* photographer Stephen Wayda], and they're fine, but I hated doing them. I had a cold. And then they were supposed to only be for the magazine, but *Playboy* leaked them to the press.'

Ultimately, Maryam felt exploited by the experience. In contrast, the same summer Timothy Dalton appeared on the cover of *Playgirl*, a magazine featuring male nudity. Dalton did not pose for any photos – clothed or unclothed (the magazine used studio publicity shots). He only granted an interview.

Carey Lowell faced the same choice as d'Abo, and she held no illusions about how it could impact her career. 'I have never been hungry in terms of acting. I've never been really ambitious ... We had to go into the St James Hotel in Los Angeles and do this press conference with a big audience. Some reporter raised his hand and said, "So are you going to do *Playboy*?" and I said, "No." ... If I was ambitious and if I had been thinking, that would have been the next step.'

Lowell also looks back on her choice with mixed emotions. 'In some ways I only regretted it because I thought, boy my body was really great then and I wish it had been captured for posterity. But, you know, I have the home pictures.'

Despite the sexual politics of the Eighties, the Bond Girls of the era have stayed in the public eye. Personalities like Grace Jones and Barbara Carrera have remained in the limelight. Others, like Kim Basinger and Carey Lowell, have gone on to more prominent roles in movies and television. Basinger, of course, won an Oscar for Best Actress in a Supporting Role in 1997 for *L.A. Confidential*. Talisa Soto has worked consistently in films since 1989, including a wonderful performance in *Piñero* with Benjamin Bratt and securing a measure of fame with a recurring role in the *Mortal Kombat* series.

Even those who have left work in front of the camera have certainly not faded into obscurity. Carole Ashby produced a documentary in 2000 and soon after opened a nightclub in London. Fiona Fullerton left film and stage work when she had children, but she still enjoys the cachet Bond offers. 'James [my son], although he would never admit this, scores very highly in the classroom because his mummy was in a Bond movie. And often I'll get his little friends coming, sidling up to me and say, "Were you really in a Bond film?" And I say, "Yes, I was." They go, "Hah! Which one?" I get other mums and dads coming up to me at the school gate saying, "Oh, we had to rent your video the other day because little Charlie insisted."'

In the Nineties, a mood seemed to settle that women could celebrate their sexuality on their own terms. They could have power and be provocative without being mere props in male fantasies. There was a decidedly feminine look back at the sexuality of the Fifties and Sixties with kinky models like Betty Page becoming fashion icons for women, and with Madonna (a future Bond woman) publishing her *Sex* book. When, after a six-year absence, Bond returned to the screen in the form of Pierce Brosnan, the attitudes of women towards portraying sexuality seemed to have shifted. The Bond filmmakers helped define that shift.

Up until Brosnan's debut in *GoldenEye*, women had limited input on the Bond films. Screenwriter Johanna Harwood helped craft the first two Bond films, but she was the last female 007 screenwriter for thirty-six years. Although Dana Broccoli was a silent partner to her husband, producer Cubby Broccoli, her voice was important. Many actresses remember that she was often part of the casting process. 'I worked very closely with Cubby all through the years,' Broccoli recalls 'And I think I might have [contributed to the way some of the women were portrayed], but we had a great team of people working on the films you know.'

During the Eighties, Cubby and Dana Broccoli's daughter Barbara followed in the footsteps of her half-brother Michael Wilson. She began working on the Bond films, tackling various jobs and taking on greater responsibility. She also became great friends with many of the Bond Girls of the era.

When it came time to develop *GoldenEye*, Barbara Broccoli joined her brother Michael as producer. Barbara's mother, Dana says, 'I feel that Barbara's involvement in the films as co-producer has had a great impact on the way the women are portrayed. And I think that Michael Wilson and the writers welcome her input. I think it's very important to have a woman of the day to influence us.'

Carey Lowell (above) with Desmond Llewelyn (Q) and Timothy Dalton (Bond).

Carey Lowell (opposite) with Timothy Dalton relaxing off set during the filming of *Licence To Kill*.

'... I THINK YOU ARE A SEXIST, MISOGYNIST DINOSAUR, A RELIC OF THE COLD WAR'

JUDI DENCH AS M IN *GOLDENEYE*

Certainly, some things changed when Barbara Broccoli became more involved. Not only does she contribute to the script but she scrutinizes the way women are shown in posters, television commercials, documentaries and books.

Barbara herself is more reserved about her contribution to the way women are portrayed in the Bond films. 'I think I get a lot of credit which is not deserved in that regard because in my view all characters should be interesting.' Broccoli gives an example of her role in one of the most notable casting decisions involving an actress during the Brosnan era. 'In *GoldenEye*, Martin Campbell and Bruce Feirstein suggested casting M as a woman. My reaction to it was, "Okay, as long as it's not a gimmick." In fact, it wasn't until Judi Dench accepted the part that Michael and I were convinced the character of M should be played by a woman.

'We could have cast the wrong person, but with Judi Dench we were exceptionally fortunate. She brings a tremendous weight to the character of M. She doesn't play it as a woman trying to prove a point, trying to be a man. She's complex, intelligent and we knew the audiences would embrace her as 007's boss.'

Dench, the grande Dame of the British stage and the Oscar-winning film actress, loved joining the ranks of Bond women: 'The first television that I ever did was with Bernard Lee, and I was completely in awe of him. So when suddenly I was asked to play M, I was rather dumb struck. But my husband and my daughter were very excited indeed. My husband thought it was great ... I really shouldn't be called a Bond woman at all, but I call myself one.'

Samantha Bond was another important addition to the 'Bond Family' in the 1990s. She has appeared as Miss Moneypenny in all the Brosnan films and remains a busy and well-known actress on the British stage. She has starred with Dame Judi Dench in *Amy's View* and has headlined in other major productions in roles such as Lady Macbeth in *Macbeth*. In addition Samantha has a vibrant career in television and radio.

The actresses of the Nineties are still digesting their Bond experience. Izabella Scorupco backed away from the film industry for four years after *GoldenEye*. She told entertainment writer Fred Topel in 2000, 'I totally closed off ... I was confused and I think I was a little bit lost ... instead of just enjoying it.' However, she has now returned to her film career with films such as *Vertical Limit* (2000) and *Reign of Fire* (2002).

In contrast, Famke Janssen has worked continually since her turn as the thigh-crushing villainess, Xenia. Famke has had her own way of dealing with her Bond Girl baggage. In an effort to showcase the diversity of her career (such as having appeared in films directed by Woody Allen and Robert Altman), Janssen avoids interviews that focus solely on Bond. She has appeared with Halle Berry in the successful *X-Men* films and admitted to spoofing her Bond Girl image in *I Spy*.

Michelle Yeoh is the one actress everyone points to as the epitome of the strong Nineties woman. In fact, director Roger Spottiswoode declared that his film would not star a 'Bond Girl' but a 'Bond

Woman'. Clearly, Yeoh left her mark, as Halle Berry explains, 'Michelle Yeoh was incredible. She brought all her martial arts training and her feistiness that I think has set a new benchmark for women in film.' Yeoh gained plaudits for more than her ability to handle action in the acclaimed *Crouching Tiger, Hidden Dragon* (2000), but she has turned down numerous offers to appear in Western films and recently declined a cameo role in *Die Another Day*. She says, 'I want to make movies with Chinese talent and themes, to have joint East-West or all Asian productions, and do things we can be proud of.'

Sophie Marceau and Denise Richards have kept working steadily since Bond, with Marceau writing and directing her first feature in 2002.

Barbara Broccoli says, 'Many of these women are continually inundated with enquiries about being a Bond Girl. You think, "My performance is done. The film has screened. Do I have to respond to every request and question about Bond for the rest of my life?" I think actresses just want to get on with their careers and lives.'

The actresses from the Nineties have yet to experience the full force of nostalgia that builds in fans over the years and creates the steady drumbeat of attention. The Bond Girls of the decade all survived the exhausting promotional process. Yet the questions, autograph requests, and association with 007 will be with them forever.

Denise Richards (Christmas Jones in *The World Is Not Enough*) knew from the start that participating in a Bond film was something different: 'It's overwhelming to be a part of the Bond series. Just to be a part of that whole thing was very intimidating, but they all made me feel very comfortable and welcome.'

In September, 1999, many Bond women gathered for a landmark photo shoot for *Vanity Fair* magazine by Annie Leibovitz. The photo sessions took place in New York and Los Angeles, featuring Ursula Andress, Shirley Eaton, Honor Blackman, Luciana Paluzzi, Jill St John, Lana Wood, Jane Seymour, Gloria Hendry, Maud Adams, Caroline Munro, Lois Chiles, Lynn-Holly Johnson, Kristina Wayborn, Tanya Roberts, Maryam d'Abo, Carey Lowell, Talisa Soto, Michelle Yeoh and Denise Richards. For the women who gathered, a sense of sisterhood quickly developed. Some knew each other. Others quickly felt as though they should know each other better. They had all shared something intangible, an experience that was unique for each but transforming for all.

As Dana Broccoli, who has known virtually every actress to appear in the EON-produced Bond movies, comments, 'Every Bond actress I've ever known has always told me that being a Bond Girl changed her life forever ... it's like being a member of a very exclusive club where they had been through the tremendous pressure of the Bond film world, which kind of binds them all together.'

Famke Janssen (Xenia in *GoldenEye*) felt being in a Bond film would give her the chance to make a mark by being different. She wanted to give a performance 'that would set it apart from the other Bond women in the past.' She ultimately felt the effort was worth it. 'I fought a lot in terms of keeping what I thought was essential in the character and I think it was worth the whole struggle.'

'TO BE A STRONG WOMAN AND TO BE TAKEN SERIOUSLY TODAY DOESN'T MEAN THAT YOU HAVE TO LOSE YOUR SENSE OF FEMININITY'

HALLE BERRY AS JINX IN *DIE ANOTHER DAY*

In 2002, the Bond Girls of *Die Another Day* – Halle Berry and Rosamund Pike – emerged in the new millennium fully realized. The modern Bond woman was an icon not just for magazines like *Playboy* and *Esquire* but for *Vogue* and *Cosmopolitan*. She was at peace with herself and her role in popular culture. Rosamund Pike comments, 'It's a label you're proud to carry.' She adds, without worrying about a distinction between 'Bond Woman' and 'Bond Girl', 'Miranda Frost is a Bond Girl and is always going to be a Bond Girl.'

They saw the scripts, breathed life into the words, and didn't feel a disconnection between sex, beauty, strength, power and intellect. They are aided by a publicity department run by two women who understand the fine balance that attracts both sexes to these characters.

Anne Bennett, who has worked on the Bond films with former distributor UIP and now manages publicity for EON Productions, acknowledges the constant battle. 'While we as the production company and the producers have tried to change the perception of women in the Bond films, I think the media still try to concentrate on what their perception is, i.e. as sex symbols.'

Bennett saw the 'astounding' beauty in the image of Halle Berry in her orange bikini, but she also recognized that the image needed to be balanced with the character's chief appeal – her equality with Bond.

That concern with the image of how the women are portrayed translates into subtle shifts in the way the media judges the more recent Bond Girls. Anne Bennett and Barbara Broccoli can complain – and do – that the media continues to portray the characters and actresses in the Bond films as sex objects. Nonetheless, the world does notice when a film has two female cast members who both earn Oscar nominations for Best Actress (Judi Dench for *Iris* and Halle Berry for *Monsters Ball*), and one of those actresses wins the Academy Award. Because the filmmaking team has made clear to the world their respect for the talents of women like Berry and Dench, the media and the public has reassessed Bond Girls.

Men, whether they be Sean Connery, John Wayne or Harrison Ford, have been able, in the past, to move between genres with greater ease than women. For example it took years of work before Diana Rigg earned the acclaim she deserved for her stage work in London. Women, led by the likes of Halle Berry, Sophie Marceau and Famke Janssen, are demanding the same creative freedom, not just by raising their voices, but by proving their talent. When asked at the start of a production press conference for *Die Another Day* why she accepted a role in a Bond film now she was established as a top actress, Berry does not hesitate to answer. 'I've suffered a lot in my career by not being taken seriously from the beginning. So I would never have frowned upon a Bond movie for those reasons. I've always felt good about my sexuality and about being a woman, and everything that encompasses being a woman. I started off as a model and in beauty pageants, so I've always embraced that side of womanhood, and I've tried to have a career that was very diverse. There are times when I used that part of who I am to the hilt, and there are times when I chose to take on more character roles, and I sort of shed that part of myself. So I've been fortunate in a way, and have been able to find the balance. I think it's really important. I've been teaching my daughter those very same values, that to be a strong woman and to be taken seriously today doesn't mean that you have to lose your sense of femininity, and lose all the things that make women so much different from men, and so wonderful. That's the gift that we, as women, have.'

Ever since 1962, the world has been captivated by the actresses who have shared the adventures of James Bond. Their beauty and sexuality has excited us. Their strength and independence has challenged us. Over four decades they have fought for their own identity but always with grace and humour. Just as Bond is forever part of their lives, these actresses are forever part of film history.

A P P E N D I X

A comprehensive register of actresses who have appeared in the James Bond film series.
Compiled by Tim Greaves, with thanks to Meg Simmonds at Eon Productions.

DR. NO (1962)
Honey Ryder — Ursula Andress
Miss Taro — Zena Marshall
Sylvia Trench — Eunice Gayson
Miss Moneypenny — Lois Maxwell
Girl Photographer — Marguerite LeWars
Sister Lily — Yvonne Shima
Sister Rose — Michel Mok
Mary — Dolores Keator
Uncredited
Professor Dent's Secretary — Bettine Le Beau
Jamaican Hotel Receptionist — Malou Pantera

FROM RUSSIA WITH LOVE (1963)
Tatiana Romanava — Daniela Bianchi
(Colonel) Rosa Klebb — Lotte Lenya
Sylvia Trench — Eunice Gayson
Kerim's Girl — Nadja Regin
Miss Moneypenny — Lois Maxwell
Vida — Aliza Gur
Zora — Martine Beswick
Gypsy Dancer — Leila Guiraut
Grant's Masseuse — Jan Williams

GOLDFINGER (1964)
Pussy Galore — Honor Blackman
Jill Masterson — Shirley Eaton
Tilly Masterson — Tania Mallet
Miss Moneypenny — Lois Maxwell
Bonita — Nadja Regin
Sydney — Tricia Muller
Dink — Margaret Nolan
Mei-Lei — Mai Ling
Swiss Gatekeeper — Varley Thomas
Uncredited
Miami Hotel Maid — Janette Rowsell
Flying Circus Pilots — Aleta Morrison
Maggie Wright
Jane Holland
Jane Murdoch
Maise Farrell
Caron Gardner
Lesley Hill

THUNDERBALL (1965)
Domino Derval — Claudine Auger
Fiona Volpe — Luciana Paluzzi
Paula Caplan — Martine Beswick
Patricia Fearing — Mollie Peters
Miss Moneypenny — Lois Maxwell
Madame Boitier — Rose Alba
Uncredited
Mademoiselle LaPorte — Maryse Guy Mitsouko
Dance Partner — Diane Hartford
Prue — Suzy Kendall

YOU ONLY LIVE TWICE (1967)
Aki — Akiko Wakabayashi
Kissy — Mie Hama
Helga Brandt — Karin Dor
Miss Moneypenny — Lois Maxwell
Ling — Tsai Chin
Bond's Masseuse — Jeanne Roland
Uncredited
Bath Girls — Mai Ling
Yee-Wah Yang
Yasuko Nagazumi

CASINO ROYALE (1967)
Vesper Lynd — Ursula Andress
Mata Bond — Joanna Pettet
The Detainer — Daliah Lavi
Agent Mimi — Deborah Kerr
Miss Moneypenny — Barbara Bouchet
Buttercup — Angela Scoular
Eliza — Gabriella Licudi
Heather — Tracey Crisp
Peg — Elaine Taylor
Miss Goodthighs — Jacky Bisset
Meg — Alexandra Bastedo
Frau Hoffner — Anna Quayle
FANG Leader — Tracy Reed
Control Girl — Penny Riley
Captain of the Guards — Jeanne Roland

ON HER MAJESTY'S SECRET SERVICE (1969)
(Comtessa) Teresa Di Vicenzo (Tracy) — Diana Rigg
Irma Bunt — Ilse Steppat
Miss Moneypenny — Lois Maxwell
Ruby Bartlett — Angela Scoular
Olympe — Virginia North
Nancy — Catherina Von Schell
American Guest (Casino) — Bessie Love
The Piz Gloria Girls
Scandinavian — Julie Ege
English — Joanna Lumley
Irish — Jenny Hanley
Australian — Anouska Hempel
German — Ingrit Back
Chinese — Mona Chong
American — Dani Sheridan
Indian — Zara
Jamaican — Sylvana Henriques
Israeli — Helena Ronee

DIAMONDS ARE FOREVER (1971)
Tiffany Case — Jill St John
Plenty O'Toole — Lana Wood
Mrs Whistler — Margaret Lacey
Miss Moneypenny — Lois Maxwell
Uncredited
Bambi — Lola Larson
Thumper — Trina Parks
Marie — Denise Perrier
Whyte House Showgirls — Cassandra Peterson
Valerie Perrine

LIVE AND LET DIE (1973)
Solitaire — Jane Seymour
Rosie Carver — Gloria Hendry
Miss Moneypenny — Lois Maxwell
Mrs Bell — Ruth Kempf
Miss Caruso — Madeline Smith
Oh Cult Sales Girl — Kubi Chaza
Fillet of Soul Singer — B. J. Arnau

THE MAN WITH THE GOLDEN GUN (1974)
Mary Goodnight — Britt Ekland
Andrea Anders — Maud Adams
Miss Moneypenny — Lois Maxwell
Saida — Carmen Sautoy
Uncredited
Chew Mee — Francoise Thilly
Hip's Nieces
Cha — Joie Vejjijiva
Nara — Cheung Chuen Nam
Bottom's Up Hostess — Wei Wei Wong

THE SPY WHO LOVED ME (1977)
(Major) Anya Amasova — Barbara Bach
Naomi — Caroline Munro
Miss Moneypenny — Lois Maxwell
Felicca — Olga Bisera
Hotel Receptionist — Valerie Leon
Log Cabin Girl — Sue Vanner
Rubelvitch — Eva Rueber-Staier
Stromberg's Assistant — Marilyn Galsworthy
Arab Beauties — Felicity York
Dawn Rodrigues
Anika Pavel
Jill Goodall

MOONRAKER (1979)
(Dr) Holly Goodhead — Lois Chiles
Corinne Dufour — Corinne Clery
Miss Moneypenny — Lois Maxwell
Manuela — Emily Bolton
Dolly — Blanche Ravalec
Apollo Stewardess — Leila Shenna
Jungle Beauty — Irka Bochenko
Museum Guide — Anne Lonnberg
Gogol's Girl — Lizzie Warville
Countess Lubinski — Catherine Serre
Signorina Del Mateo — Chichinou Kaeppler
Lady Victoria Devon — Francoise Gayat
Mademoiselle Deradier — Beatrice Libert
Drax Girls — Christina Hui
Nicaise Jean Louis

FOR YOUR EYES ONLY (1981)

Melina Havelock	Carole Bouquet
Bibi Dahl	Lynn-Holly Johnson
(Countess) Lisl Von Schlaf	Cassandra Harris
Jacoba Brink	Jill Bennett
Miss Moneypenny	Lois Maxwell
Iona Havelock	Toby Robins
Rublevich	Eva Rueber-Staier
Flower Shop Sales Girl	Robbin Young
The Prime Minister	Janet Brown
Uncredited	
Sharon (Q's Assistant)	Maureen Bennett
Casino Girl	Max Vesterhalt
Bond Beauties	Kim Mills
	Lizzie Warville
	Lalla Dean
	Evelyn Drogue
	Laoura Hadzivageli
	Koko
	Chai Lee
	Tula
	Vanya
	Viva
	Alison Worth

OCTOPUSSY (1983)

Octopussy	Maud Adams
Magda	Kristina Wayborn
Miss Moneypenny	Lois Maxwell
Penelope Smallbone	Michaela Clavell
Gwendoline	Suzanne Jerome
Midge	Cherry Gillespie
Bianca	Tina Hudson
Rublevitch	Eva Rueber-Staier
Schatzl	Brenda Cowling
Circus Performers	Carol Richter
	Vera and Shirley Fossett
The Octopussy Girls	Mary Stavin
	Carolyn Seaward
	Carole Ashby
	Cheryl Anne
	Jani-Z
	Julie Martin
	Joni Flynn
	Julie Barth
	Kathy Davies
	Helene Hunt
	Gillian De Terville
	Safira Afzal
	Louise King
	Tina Robinson
	Alison Worth
	Janine Andrews
	Lynda Knight
Gymnasts	Suzanne Dando
	Teresa Craddock
	Kirsten Harrison
	Christine Cullers
	Lisa Jackman
	Jane Aldridge
	Christine Gibson
	Sumisha Hassani
	Tracy Llewellyn
	Susan Cheesebrough
	Barbara Mould
	Eileen Ward
	Ruth Flynn
Uncredited	
Q's Assistant	Lorraine Fraiser
Woman in Phonebooth	Patricia Marks
Indian Hotel Girl	Marta Gillot

NEVER SAY NEVER AGAIN (1983)

Domino Petachi	Kim Basinger
Fatima Blush	Barbara Carrera
Miss Moneypenny	Pamela Salem
Patricia	Prunella Gee
Nicole	Saskia Cohen Tanugi
Shrublands Nurse	Lucy Hornak
Shrublands Cook	Joanna Dickens
Lady in Bahamas	Valerie Leon
French Minister	Sylvia Marriott
Health Spa Receptionist	Jill Meager
Masseuse	Brenda Kempner
Girl Hostage	Wendy Leech

A VIEW TO A KILL (1985)

Stacey Sutton	Tanya Roberts
May Day	Grace Jones
Pola Ivanova	Fiona Fullerton
Jenny Flex	Alison Doody
Pan Ho	Papillon Soo Soo
Miss Moneypenny	Lois Maxwell
Kimberley Jones	Mary Stavin
Dominique (Whistling Girl)	Carole Ashby
The Girls	Sian Adey-Jones
	Nike Clark
	Gloria Douse

The Girls (continued)

	Caroline Hallett
	Elke Ritschel
	Lou-Anne Ronchi
	Paula Thomas
	Mayako Torigai
Uncredited	
	Celine Cawley
	Helen Clitherow
	Samina Afzal
	Maggie Defreitas
	Deborah Hanna
	Josanne Haydon-Pearce
	Ann Jackson
	Terri Johns
	Karen Loughlin
	Angela Lyn
	Patricia Martinez
	Kim Ashfield Norton
	Helen Smith
	Jane Spencer
	Toni White

THE LIVING DAYLIGHTS (1987)

Kara Milovy	Maryam d'Abo
Miss Moneypenny	Caroline Bliss
Rubavitch	Virginia Hey
Rosika Miklos	Julie T. Wallace
Liz	Catherine Rabett
Ava	Duliece Liecier
Linda (Yacht Girl)	Kell Tyler
The Girls	Odette Benatar
	Femi Gardiner
	Mayte Sanchez
	Dianna Casale
	Patricia Keefer
	Cela Savannah
	Waris Walsh
	Sharon Devlin
	Ruddy Rodriguez
	Karen Seeberg
	Karen Williams

LICENCE TO KILL (1989)

Pam Bouvier	Carey Lowell
Lupe Lamora	Talisa Soto
Della Churchill	Priscilla Barnes
Miss Moneypenny	Caroline Bliss
Loti	Diana Lee-Hsu
Barrelhead Stripper	Jeannine Bisignano
Consuelo	Cynthia Fallon
Ticket Agent	Teresa Blake
Barrelhead Waitress	Edna Bolkan

GOLDENEYE (1995)

Natalya Fyodorovna Simonova	Izabella Scorupco
Xenia Sergeyevna Onatopp	Famke Janssen
M	Judi Dench
Miss Moneypenny	Samantha Bond
Caroline	Serena Gordon
Irina	Minnie Driver
Anna	Michelle Arthur

TOMORROW NEVER DIES (1997)

Wai Lin	Michelle Yeoh
Paris Carver	Teri Hatcher
M	Judi Dench
Miss Moneypenny	Samantha Bond
(Professor) Inga Bergstrom	Cecilie Thomsen
Tamara Steel	Nina Young
Carver's PR Lady	Daphne Deckers
Staff Officer 2	Laura Brattan
Beth Davidson	Nadia Cameron
Mary Golson	Liza Ross
Uncredited	
Avis Agent	Antje Schmidt

THE WORLD IS NOT ENOUGH (1999)

Elektra King	Sophie Marceau
(Dr) Christmas Jones	Denise Richards
Cigar Girl	Maria Grazia Cucinotta
M	Judi Dench
Miss Moneypenny	Samantha Bond
(Dr) Molly Warmflash	Serena Scott Thomas
Nina	Daisy Beaumont
Verushka	Nina Muschallik

DIE ANOTHER DAY (2002)

Giacinta Johnson (Jinx)	Halle Berry
Miranda Frost	Rosamund Pike
M	Judi Dench
Miss Moneypenny	Samantha Bond
Peaceful Fountains of Desire	Rachel Grant
Air Hostess	Deborah Moore
Korean Scorpion Guard	Tymarah
Nurse	Cristina Contes
Buckingham Palace Reporter	Ami Chorlton
Uncredited	
Verity	Madonna

ACKNOWLEDGEMENTS

Like the James Bond films, this book was a collaborative effort. Literally dozens of individuals helped shape the final product. Below are a few of the names the authors would like to thank.

At EON Productions: Michael G. Wilson, Barbara Broccoli, David G. Wilson, Jenni McMurrie, Meg Simmonds, Anne Bennett, Katherine McCormack, David Pope, Keith Snelgrove, Michael Tavares, John Parkinson and so many others in the company have made our tangential association with Bond over the years a wonderful experience.

We want to thank Dana Broccoli separately. She is the sparkle in the Bond diamond, and her insights and generosity made this book so much richer. We'd also like to thank Lori Kustich who works with Mrs. Broccoli for her help.

Maryam would like to pay special tribute to the Bond alumni who participated in her documentary *Bond Girls Are Forever*: Ursula Andress, Honor Blackman, Luciana Paluzzi, Jill St. John, Maud Adams, Lois Chiles, Carey Lowell, Dame Judi Dench, Samantha Bond, Halle Berry, and Rosamund Pike. In addition, she wants to pay thanks to Shirley Eaton, Caroline Monroe, Sean Connery, George Lazenby, Roger Moore, Timothy Dalton and Pierce Brosnan, all of whom supported the documentary.

John Cork would like to thank all the Bond women whom he has had the opportunity to meet and interview over the years. In particular, Lynn-Holly Johnson, Nikki van der Zyl, Barbara Jefford, Marguerite LeWars and Gloria Hendry helped considerably at the last minute.

Much of the writing of this book was done under the roof of Andrew Lycett's home in London, one of Britain's great biographers. His hospitality and inspiration meant a tremendous amount to this project. Mark, Heather, Jack and Chesney Clubb, as always, came to the aide of the party in unexpected ways.

Additional support and background came from Peter Janson-Smith, Lili Pohlmann, Iain Johnstone, Sam Peffer, Lindy Hemming, Emma Porteous, Neal Purvis and Robert Wade, and Bruce Feirstein. George Martin went to great effort to provide original interview material with Halle Berry and Rosamund Pike. Bruce Scivally, Michael Monahan, Scott McIsaac, Tom Wendler, Michael VanBlaricum, Brad Frank, Jeff Kehoe, Marcie Levin, James Burkart Jr. and Jim Kroeper all helped as well. Without the help of Editorial Consultant Tim Greaves, John Cork could not have undertaken this project, and thus John offers a special thanks for Tim's generous commitment of time and energy.

Maryam d'Abo's work on this project came out of her documentary produced through Planet Grande Productions where John Watkins and John Fitzgerald (among others) gave great assistance. Also, thanks to Gillian Gordon, Howard Rosenman, Barry Tyerman and Hugh Hudson for their unwavering support.

Boxtree invited us to work on this book, and everyone there, particularly Gordon Wise, Emma Marriott and Natalie Jerome, handled the schedule, content and pressures with grace and aplomb. No one could ask for a better team. Dave Breen's elegant design has made this tome a dream to behold.

PHOTO CREDITS